THE
EDUCATION
OF A
HORSEPLAYER

by

SAM (THE GENIUS) LEWIN

with

FREDERICK C. KLEIN

A Stuart L. Daniels Book

A POWERS & LEIGHTON PUBLICATION

1978 EDITION

Published by
Melvin Powers
WILSHIRE BOOK COMPANY
12015 Sherman Road
No. Hollywood, California 91605
Telephone: (213) 875-1711

To my son
Gregg Leo Lewin

Printed by

HAL LEIGHTON PRINTING CO.
P.O. Box 1231
Beverly Hills, California 90213
Telephone: (213) 983-1105

The publisher acknowledges with thanks the material appearing herein from *The Morning Telegraph*. This material is not to be reproduced without the permission of the copyright owner, Triangle Publications, Inc.

First Edition: 1969

"Published by arrangement with Hawthorn Books, Inc."

ISBN 0-87980-244-8

Contents

Contents

1

Nobody's a Genius

Around the race tracks they call me The Genius. Now, I'll cheerfully admit to having picked an unusually large number of winners in my forty years in racing, and to taking many thousands of dollars out of the game. What's more, my ego is as big as the next man's—a lot of people will tell you it's bigger.

But I'm not really a genius. My wife, Frances, says that the only genius at the track is the guy who picked the winner in the race that was just run, and I agree. It was difficult enough coming out ahead financially in the days when the legal bookmakers took their bets on the New York lawns and arranged the odds so they could keep 5 percent as their commission; it's far, far more difficult today when the bettor gets back only about 85 cents on the dollar in winnings after the track and state take their cuts.

In 1928, when I started betting on the horses seriously, there were about 8,000 thoroughbred race horses active in the United States. By 1967, there were about 42,000 horses racing. Between 1957 and 1967 the number of races run in the United States rose from about 35,000 to 48,000. Today there are many more tracks, more owners, more trainers, more jockeys, more everything than there used to be. Add that to all the other variables the horse-player must face in every race—track conditions, post positions, weights, past performances of the animals, the odds on the board and the abilities of the horsemen—and you get some idea why there's so much truth to the saying that you might be able to beat a race, but it's tough to beat the races. In brief, don't look for easy answers when it comes to figuring how horses will run.

Despite this caveat, I think the story of how I came to be called The Genius is worth telling, not because it makes me look smart but because it's a good illustration of why the term shouldn't be used loosely in racing.

The Famous Fatty Anderson

It was in the early 1930's at the Rockingham Park race track in New Hampshire that I met William Tecumseh (Fatty) Anderson, a Californian who trained, owned and bet on horses. Fatty was a huge man physically—he was over six feet tall and weighed more than 300 pounds. His typical breakfast consisted of a dozen eggs, a pound of bacon, a gallon of coffee and a gallon of ice cream. Between such meals, he carried in his cheek with surprising dignity a lump of chewing tobacco proportionate to his size.

Fatty's knowledge of the racing game was as large as his appetite. He was a fine judge of horses and horseplayers. He knew well the vanity of bettors and the lure of larceny, both of which play so large a part in racing. He knew how to use them to his own advantage.

Then, as now, the most common type of race at any track was the claiming race, in which competition is equalized by the requirement that owners put price tags on horses they wish to enter and offer them for sale to any other owner with a horse racing at the meeting. Races are organized for horses of similar value. A horse worth $25,000, for instance, should easily win a race for $5,000 horses, but it is doubtful that the owner would take the risk of having his horse "claimed" (that is, purchased) for so cheap a price for the sake of a single victory. Or so the theory goes.

Fatty Anderson, however, knew that human vanity made the theory and practice of the claiming race something different. He knew that most trainers and owners tended to overvalue their younger horses. By racing his young horses at their proper worth Fatty won many a purse and many a bet. A Fatty Anderson horse in a $5,000 claiming race for two-year-olds was worth $5,000. More often than not, it was up against a bunch of $2,500 horses whose owners wouldn't admit that they had such cheap animals in their barns.

Fatty also knew how to play on the basic larceny in the hearts of bettors. When the average horse-owner wants to try to win a bet with an established claiming horse—one whose value has been firmly set in his races—he might risk a slight drop in the claiming price, usually 20 percent or less. Fatty, when he thought the situation was right, would take a $20,000 horse and throw him in for $8,000. He knew that the average bettor, seeing a drop in price, would immediately look for a motive; possibly that Fatty was putting a lame horse into a race in the hope it would be claimed in order to salvage a small part of his investment. Fatty *did* do that once in a while, but usually he'd simply want to win a bet on one of his horses. "They'll never believe this one," he'd chuckle when he got ready to pull off one of his coups.

Naturally, Fatty's horses didn't always win. As bettors and horsemen caught on to his methods he found it increasingly difficult to get good odds on horses he dropped in price, or to keep them from being claimed. Fatty's type of manipulation is far less prevalent today than it was in the 1930s. Later in his career, Fatty concentrated on racing high-quality horses for large purses. Nevertheless, betting remained the name of the game for Fatty. "Horses," he said, "are to win bets with."

I first ran into Fatty Anderson at the Rockingham Park Hotel, a big ramshackle wooden building near the New Hampshire track. I suppose our friendship was unusual because I was in my twenties and just getting started in the game while he was in his forties or fifties and well-established. In addition, he was a loner and didn't warm up to people easily. However, soon after we met we began talking racing, which is all real racing people ever talk about. My knowledge of the game didn't begin to match his, but I was glib and opinionated, and, I suppose, amusing to him. In addition, I was a very lucky bettor at the time, and racing people like to be around luck.

Fatty took me under his wing and we began traveling together. For several years we hit the tracks in New England and New York in summer and the Florida tracks in winter. Most of what I know about claiming, managing and betting on horses I learned from Fatty. He also taught me the joys of good food.

It was in the spring of 1937 that Fatty had a horse in his stable named Carlovinian. I thought Carlovinian was a good horse, but Fatty had an uncharacteristic blind spot about him. He kept entering him in races he couldn't win. One day at New York's Belmont Park I told Fatty that I liked his horse and thought I'd found a race for him—a $3,500 claiming race the next week for maidens. A maiden is a horse, male or female, that has never won a race. Fatty didn't take me too seriously and asked how much I thought the horse was worth. I said $4,500. He told me I'd bought a horse.

I entered Carlovinian in the race. Because I was new to the New York tracks, with no reputation for running winners, the horse went off at the generous odds of 3–1. If Fatty had saddled him, the odds would have been 6–5 or 7–5, such was his reputation at the time. I bet $200 on Carlovinian to win. Fatty looked at the odds, liked them, and went for about $15,000, not an unusual bet for him.

Carlovinian won from here to Chicago. Fatty, of course, was very happy with his winnings. After the race, while we were having dinner, he began calling me a genius. I guess he liked the sound of that nickname, because he called me that from then on. Soon the name caught on. "Here come Fatty and The Genius," people would say when we appeared at the tracks.

You can figure out if that race qualified me as a genius. The horse cost me $4,500. He was purchased in that race and I was paid the $3,500 claiming price. I won a $1,200 purse and $600 on my bet, so I was ahead $800. Fatty collected $45,000 on his bet. No wonder he thought I was a genius.

A Childhood View of Racing

I didn't set out to be a genius or a horseplayer. I was born in 1906 in Paterson, New Jersey, across the Hudson River from

New York City. Paterson then was a major silk and textile center. My father, Leo, was a manufacturer of textile machinery. He made a very good thing of his business and became quite rich. For a pastime he would bet on the horses.

I was a teen-ager before I paid much attention to that.

Jerry Kaplan, a thin, nervous little guy who lived around the corner from us in Paterson, was Dad's bookmaker. When I started high school Dad thought I was old enough to share his hobby and he began sending me over to Jerry's place in the late afternoon to ask about the horses he'd bet on. Jerry would usually say, "Tell your poppa his horse was out of the money."

After a couple of months of this I asked Dad what "out of the money" meant. Like most kids, I knew plenty about baseball, but nothing about horse racing. My dad explained that "out of the money" meant a horse didn't finish first, second or third, and thus didn't reward any of the people who bet on him.

I was astounded that a man as smart as my father was picking so many losers. I said, "All those horses you bet on—they never seem to finish first, second or third." He said, "Go on, get out of here. What do you know about horses? I win a lot." He didn't win very often, but like all horseplayers the bets he won would stick in his mind. He'd forget about all the others.

The more I thought about my father's lack of success at picking winning horses, the more interested in the game I became. I started reading the racing results in *The New York Times,* which was delivered to our house every morning. After several weeks of this, it occurred to me that I was doing things backward. I began reading the entries for the day's races, along with whatever information on the horses the paper carried, and I would guess which horses I thought would win. Then I'd check the next day to see how I'd done. Since there wasn't much prerace information in the paper I usually didn't do very well.

One spring day, when I was 18, I came home from school just in time to see my father getting into his car to go to the track. Knowing that I'd started to take an interest in the game, he asked if I wanted to go along. I did.

That day the races were at the Empire City Race Track in Yonkers, New York. Today, Yonkers Raceway, a harness-racing track, is on that same site. Yonkers was way out in the country— a real journey in those days. I remember that it was a nice day and a pleasant drive.

It was before the days of pari-mutuel machine-betting in New York. Bookmakers, fully legal and licensed, would stand on the lawns near the grandstand and take bets right out in the open. Each bookmaker had a board on which were chalked the odds on the next race. Each bookie was accompanied by a "sheet writer" —a fellow who would make a note of every bet placed. No money would change hands between the bookmaker and his customers; it was all done on credit. A bookmaker would either have to know you or be properly introduced to you before he would take your bet. The accounts would be settled at the end of the day, week or month, depending on the arrangement between customer and bookmaker.

The legal bookmakers of the 1920s were substantial men of finance, much as they are today in England, where private book-making on athletic events is still legal. One prominent New York bookmaker was Tim Mara, who later owned the New York Giants professional football team. Among others were Tom Shaw and Frank Cavanaugh, both of whom emerged from racing as rich men. Individual bookies like Mara, Shaw and Cavanaugh could handle several hundred thousand dollars in bets on a single day from their own capital. It was a demanding trade and their business prospered or fell on their ability to manipulate odds and wagers to satisfy their patrons and retain a profit for themselves.

The coming of the mutuel machines opened racing to the general public, which was all to the good. At the same time the mutuels took some of the color out of betting. Too many tracks today have the atmosphere of a supermarket on a Saturday morning.

On that first day at the track, of course, I was too young to bet. Rather, I was like a kid at his first circus. I took in everything—the crowds, the color, the excitement. The track was full of well-dressed people and jockeys in bright silk riding uniforms. I liked everything I saw. It brought to life the names and events I'd been reading about in the papers, and it was far more exciting than I'd imagined.

That day at Empire City I noticed especially that a lot of people carried and constantly referred to a newspaper called the *Morning Telegraph*. Unlike other daily papers, it was devoted almost exclusively to racing and carried detailed information on race entries and results.

The very next day I bought a copy of the *Telegraph*. It was then that my serious study of racing began. While other kids spent their allowance money on movies and sodas, I bought the *Telegraph* with mine.

Late that same summer of 1924, a French horse, Epinard, came to Belmont Park to run in one of the first big international races ever held in the United States. The papers—the regular dailies as well as the *Telegraph*—were full of news about the race. Like most horseplayers, my father was impressed with the sportswriters' opinions of horses. Based on what he'd read, he had already made up his mind to bet on Epinard. He thought—he knew!—that Epinard was the greatest horse in the world.

I looked up the past-performance records of the horses entered in that race. One horse impressed me, and that was Wise Counsellor. For all his races, the *Morning Telegraph* listed almost nothing but "ones" after his name. Then, as now, it kept track of a horse's position at various points in a race—at the quarter-mile, the half, three-quarters, and so forth. The "ones" meant Wise Counsellor was in first place in the early portions of many of his races. That was the main thing I noticed then—early speed. I didn't know anything about "pace" in a race, or what is known as "class" in horses. All I looked for were those "ones." That's all a lot of people who fancy themselves as very smart horseplayers still look for when they try to determine the outcome of a race.

I showed Dad all the "ones" next to Wise Counsellor. Rather timidly I pointed out that the final running times Wise Counsellor had recorded in his recent races compared favorably with those of Epinard. I asked if Wise Counsellor didn't look like a better bet than Epinard.

"What do you know about horses?" my dad said. "Epinard is the greatest horse in the world; all the newspapers say so. He can't lose."

Dad placed his bet on Epinard. At about 5:30 P.M. he sent me to Jerry Kaplan's place to get the race results. Jerry ticked off the order of finish in the day's early races, but I was too impatient to listen. "Who won the big race?" I asked, holding my breath. "Wise Counsellor . . . Epinard was second," he said. I knew now how it felt to pick a winner. It felt wonderful.

It still didn't occur to me to actually bet on horses. It's one thing to pick winners for fun, but backing your judgment with money is something else. It's that way with a lot of games. I played a lot of pool as a kid, and there were guys who could beat me every time when nothing was on the line. Put a few dollars on the game, though, and they would choke up. That's true with golf, cards, bowling, flipping cards into a hat, anything you'd care to name. It's especially true in horse racing. It takes courage to support your calculations on a race with cash from your own pocket. It also takes a good deal of knowledge to manage your money so that you get the most out of it. As I will explain in detail later, the way you handle your money at the track is nearly as important in winning as the quality of your handicapping. You will have to supply the courage yourself.

After graduation from high school, I went directly into law school. In those days a college degree wasn't a requirement for law school as it is in many places today. My parents wanted me to be either a lawyer or a doctor and never spared the opportunity to tell me so. The law looked like the least painful of the two professions, so I enrolled in the New Jersey Law School in Newark.

Some others from Paterson also went to law school, so we formed a car pool to drive to Newark each morning. It took about 45 minutes for the 14-mile trip, and on the way I'd read the *Morning Telegraph*. When my friends would ask about the paper I'd imply that I was a great horseplayer by pointing out things about the horses. I told them what a great bettor I was, even though I'd never made a bet. As it turned out, I picked winners almost every day, and my friends were impressed. It wasn't long before one of the fellows suggested that we capitalize on my talents by going to the races in Maryland, where they had pari-mutuel betting and credit with a bookmaker wasn't necessary. With all of my boasting, I couldn't very well have refused.

In racing, as in other aspects of life, there's beginner's luck. I can't explain what it is or what causes it; I just know that I had it in abundance. Almost everyone who has tried to make a go of betting was encouraged by beginner's luck, pure and simple. Without it, they never would have continued in the game.

For some people beginner's luck dries up suddenly and they dry up with it. Others manage to learn something along the way, and when their early luck goes they have a residue of knowledge to carry them on. Such people are few and I guess I am one of them. Later, when I explain my handicapping methods, I will be more systematic and provide information which can be put to practical use. For now, you will have to take me at my word about beginner's luck.

Having determined to go to the races, we drove all that next Friday night (no super highways then) and arrived at the Laurel Race Course, near Baltimore, just before the Saturday races were to begin. The other fellows knew nothing about racing, so they left selections to me. I fell back on the way I had picked Wise Counsellor over Epinard; I looked for "speed" horses with strings of "ones" after their names in the *Telegraph* listings. After pooling our money we had about $20 to bet on each race. We bet every which way—win only, win–show, across-the-board—whatever struck our fancy. We knew as little about managing our money as we did about the other facets of the game.

Wouldn't you know! We had a terrific day. I picked five winners. Our pool made a profit of about $1,000, of which my share was around $200. That paid for our trip, admission to the track and meals, with plenty left over. I said to myself, "This is an easy game." I couldn't understand why my dad was losing all those bets. In one day at the track I was $200 ahead, and $200 was a lot of money in those days.

The Lure of the Track

It was then that I began to lose interest in the law and neglect my studies. Instead of waiting until morning to buy the *Telegraph,* I'd get it at night and stay up late studying it. When I couldn't get to the track I'd handicap the races anyway and make imaginary bets. I would persuade my friends to go to the races just about every weekend. With all the time spent at the track, it was miraculous that so many of them finished school and became lawyers. We lost sometimes, but we won more often—enough to keep my interest at a high pitch.

I didn't say much about this at home. My folks had their hearts set on me becoming a lawyer—God forbid a horseplayer. I'd explain my trips to Maryland by saying I needed frequent rests from the grind of study. Actually, what I told them was only partly untrue, because I was studying—the horses.

However, that summer my handicapping interest did come to light. During the week I worked at Dad's factory; weekends we'd go to our summer place in Belmar on the New Jersey shore. As usual, my dad was playing the horses and losing. I would ask about the horse he was playing, and when he'd tell me, I'd usually disagree. An argument would ensue. One Saturday my dad said he'd had it with me and my opinions. "Okay, if you're so smart, I'll let you bet and we'll see how you make out."

We went to a bookmaking parlor located in the back of a stationery store in Belmar. The store was run-down, but the backroom, where bets were taken, was well-appointed. It was large and bright and filled with comfortable chairs for the bettors. A big blackboard ran all the way around the walls. The names of horses and their odds were posted on the board in chalk. There was a wire service that gave the results of races from tracks all over the country. Drinks and sandwiches were free.

Dad and I started picking, but at first he wouldn't let me bet. As usual, his horses lost while I picked a few winners. Finally, he picked up the newspaper in which I had circled my choices. In the seventh race at Arlington Park in Chicago I'd chosen a filly named Annie Ree. In those days I didn't know that a filly—a young female—had very little chance of winning over colts—young males. My dad couldn't figure out why I'd picked her. In addition to her sex handicap, she was a sprinter and the race was for 1⅛ miles. She really didn't figure to win. Today

I never would bet her under the same circumstances, but at that time I was dazzled by the "ones" after her name. She was 6–1, and I liked those odds.

Dad thought I was crazy, but he'd been losing and wanted to change his luck. Despite himself he put $100 on Annie Ree to win. As we waited for the race to begin, the odds on Annie Ree started climbing—8–1, 10–1, 15–1 and finally 20–1, the highest they were allowed to go in that establishment. My dad was getting nervous, but not me. I thought the high odds were just great. I *had* learned, even at that time, that you'll never make money always betting on favorites. You've got to make yourself like long-shots—longshots with a reasonable chance to win—as well as you like favorites. That's one of the keys to financial success in betting.

The race went the way I'd figured it. Annie Ree was ahead by 2 lengths at the quarter-mile, 3 at the half, 4 at the three-quarters and 5 at the stretch. She won easily. At the track she paid $52 on a $2 bet, or 25–1, but we were paid only $42 because of the 20–1 house limit. My dad had won $2,000 and was very happy. He slapped me on the back and said, "Study your newspaper next week, son, and next Saturday we'll come back here and do this again." And we did.

That was the way it went for me that year. The *Telegraph* every day, trips to Maryland on weekends during the school year and trips to the bookmaking place in the summer. I began to like racing more and more and the study of law less and less.

It was during the next year—my third in law school—that I took the step that launched my career in racing. My school friends and I by this time were confirmed race-goers who spent every free weekend at the tracks. When Thanksgiving vacation rolled around, we pooled $400 and went off to make a week of it at Bowie Race Course, near Baltimore.

Again my luck held. We won two or three races a day for the

first few days, enough to keep our $400 intact. On the final day I picked the winner of every race on a seven-race card. I had a bit of bad luck when one winner, Balko, was disqualified in the feature race. But that was a minor setback. Our little corporation ended the week with a profit of $12,500. My share was $2,500. If I'd known as much as I do today about handling money, we'd have won many times that amount. But that didn't concern me then. The $2,500 felt like a million.

Later that week there was a disposal sale at Bowie by the Nevada Stock Farm which was a very good stable. I had also been studying breeding and felt that I knew something about it. Among the horses listed to be sold was a yearling filly, Plumosa, sired by General Thatcher out of the mare Shamrock Green, who had been a good sprinter. There I was with $2,500 burning a hole in my pocket. I had to have that horse. I didn't know if she was worth $50 or $50,000, but I had to find out. I bought her for $1,500.

I gave Plumosa to a trainer named Frank Byers, whom I knew from the bookmaking parlor in Belmar (the bookie was married to his daughter). When I asked what he thought of Plumosa he told me she was fine, a real good filly. I later learned that all trainers tell that to new horse-owners. Being duly impressed I paid the shipping costs and a month's training fee in advance. Plumosa would spend the winter at a farm in Freehold, New Jersey.

I couldn't get back to Paterson fast enough to tell my folks that not only was I a terrific bettor but a horse-owner as well. I announced that I was quitting law school and going into racing. They hollered plenty, but I had made up my mind. That filly was going to make me rich and famous.

Freehold is 40 miles south of Paterson, and the next week I went there to visit my horse. No one was at the farm except a caretaker. My filly was standing alone in a stall and I asked him if I could let her run without a rider. He shrugged and said it was all right with him. There was snow on the ground, but I turned her out anyway. Boy, she just flew over the snow. I was thrilled. When she finished running I patted her neck, gave her a sugar cube and put her right back in her stall without walking her or rubbing her down, as you should. I went to the farm three or four times a week for the next few months, and when nobody was around I'd do the same thing with Plumosa, letting her run as she pleased and returning her to her stall without cooling her off. That sort of treatment led to injuries that ruined Plumosa's legs. She never raced. From that day to this, many trainers have had the privilege of ruining my horses, but that one I did myself.

My plan was to race Plumosa at the Rockingham Park meeting in the spring. Her injuries made that impossible, but I went to Rockingham anyway in the hope of buying another horse. I didn't find a one to purchase, but I found many to bet on. My study of the animals began to pay off. I've never been far from a race track since.

My connection with racing hasn't only been as a bettor. At Tropical Park in early 1937, when I was thirty years old, I was making my selections from a box about 20 yards to the left of the finish line. Tropical Park was set up differently then, and the short homestretch and short run into the first turn made it a great track for speed horses, which were my favorites in those days. I played and won with amazing success. In the box next to me sat one Israel Silberman, who wasn't doing nearly as well. He watched me talk about horses and pick winners (then, as now, I didn't keep my selections secret). Silberman was impressed. After a week or so of this he invited me to dinner. He told me he owned a paint company on Long Island and was very interested in racing. He wanted to start a stable and asked if I'd manage it for him. Then he wrote his name on a blank check and placed it on the table in front of me. He told me to spend whatever was needed to get ourselves into the racing business. I took the check as calmly as I could. The next day, as an official stable manager, I was off on a horse-buying trip to Hialeah Park, near Tropical, where some good stables were quartered. Because of my friendship with Fatty Anderson I knew a lot more about buying horses than I did when I had picked up Plumosa. I wanted a couple of well-bred two-year-olds who would get our new operation, the Paragon Stable, off to a good start.

At Hialeah I passed the barn of Mrs. John Hay Whitney, whose trainer was Big Jim Healey, a fine, honest man. We started talking and he mentioned that he had a good-looking two-year-old named Family Friend who was a son of Wise Counsellor, the first winner I'd ever picked. My ears perked up. Wise Counsellor had been a successful sire, and I thought it would be wonderful to own one of his colts. Big Jim brought out Family Friend, who was dark brown and very well made. He'd won twice and finished second twice in eight starts, and looked as if he could do even better. I asked Healey how much he wanted. He said he'd sell me Family Friend if I also took another two-year-old of his, Bold Turk. I could have them both for $13,000 but I couldn't have one without the other.

I guess Big Jim must have been superstitious, because Bold Turk had a lot of white on him—a white nose and white legs. There was a current superstition that horses with a lot of white never did well. Don't ask me why—that was the belief. Later, many horses with a lot of white did very well—Rex Ellsworth's Candy Spots, who won the Preakness in 1963, is a recent example. So the superstition died.

Not being superstitious, I bought both horses and took them back to Tropical Park. Family Friend was sixth in his first race for us, and Bold Turk ran second in his first start. Then I put them both in a race that was a preparation for the Viscaya Stakes. They ran 1–2, with Family Friend winning.

The next week, Family Friend gave me my first stakes victory by winning the $10,000 Viscaya at Tropical.

When the Florida season ended Mr. Silberman and I took our horses to New York. By that time we had picked up a third horse—a colt, Deserter—whom I'd claimed for $1,250 in Florida. In New York we won only one race and it was Deserter who won it. Later that year I sent Bold Turk to New England and Family Friend to Saratoga, where both won stakes races. Bold Turk, in fact, won several stakes that summer at Suffolk Downs, near Boston, and at Narragansett Park in Rhode Island. When we counted our money at the end of 1937, Paragon Stable had recorded a profit of $21,000. Any kind of profit is quite a trick for a new stable.

Early the next year I took our $21,000 and bought nineteen yearlings; to be exact, I spent $21,500. Seventeen of those nineteen horses proceeded to win at least one race in their two-year-old year, the first year that horses race. The first three horses we sent to the post at Hialeah Park won, and believe it or not each paid $21.20 on a $2 bet. Ripley put it in his column.

In that bunch of nineteen yearlings was one that might have been the best horse I ever had, a colt named Pradis. I'm certain I could have won the Kentucky Derby with that colt. He trained beautifully. He looked great. He had no tremendous early burst of speed, but he had stamina and loads of determination. He was a real "class" horse.

When I told Mr. Silberman about Pradis he couldn't wait to see him run. Two-year-olds in Florida start racing at ⅜ of a mile, but that just wasn't Pradis' distance. I wanted to save his debut for the ⅝-mile races in New York because the longer distance fit his late-running style better. Silberman would have none of this. He wanted to see this great horse of his run, and damn the distance. I said no, but he insisted. In went Pradis at ⅜ mile on the Hialeah straight course.

There were fourteen horses in the race and Pradis was four-teenth with $\frac{1}{16}$ of a mile to go, yet he rallied to finish second. It was so close you could barely call the winner. I asked Silberman if he was satisfied. He wasn't. He wanted to run Pradis again, and soon. I pleaded with him. "This is the horse everybody waits for. For God's sake, leave him alone." I was afraid that with his kind of determination Pradis might try to do something he couldn't, such as win a very short race and injure himself in the process.

Back he went at the ⅜ mile the next week, and that's just what happened. He strained a tendon leaving the gate, hurting himself badly. He *still* finished second on three legs. That's the kind of horse he was. The race ruined him. How mad I was. We put Pradis on a farm and he eventually raced again, but he never became the champion he should have.

Not long after that Silberman and I parted company in a dis-agreement over my contract. The experience soured me for some time on managing stables for other people. For the next few years I remained a bettor and an owner of my own horses. Nobody can ruin your own horses but you and your trainer, and I would keep a close eye on my trainers.

Then World War II came and late in 1942, at the age of thirty-six, I went into the army for two years, during which period I sold my horses. Believe me, after two years of Army pay (I got to be a sergeant) I didn't have much money.

In 1946 Monmouth Park opened in New Jersey and I couldn't have been happier to be back at the track. It was there that I met George Smith, owner of a textile mill. The same thing happened with Smith that had happened with Silberman. I was playing and winning. I impressed him, so he asked me to form a stable. He named it the Art-Dale Stable, after his son and daughter. We had great success winning numerous races for two years. Then Mr. George Smith became involved in some legal difficulties in connection with his textile business and down went that stable.

In 1949 I finally got lucky with business associates. I was introduced to Irving Kirschbaum, a fine gentleman from Deal, New Jersey, who owned the Carolyn-K Stable, which was named after his wife. Mr. Kirschbaum is president of National Work Clothes Company. After we became friendly he signed me to manage his stable, and I've been with him ever since. As stable manager I buy horses, supervise their breeding and choose races for them to enter. Mr. Kirschbaum is a sportsman; he's in the game for the pleasure of owning good horses and watching them run. We've won plenty of races in the ensuing years, including many stakes. During these last few years we've been concentrating on breeding, and winners often come hard that way. But Mr. Kirschbaum is willing to spend money in the hope of coming up with some really special horses. Maybe we will someday. I also own and race my own horses and get a big kick out of that.

Don't think I've neglected my betting in the years that I've been managing stables for other people. As I've said, when my beginner's luck ran out I had learned enough to keep going on skill. After a number of years at the tracks I learned the maxim I follow today: *Pace makes the race.* I'll discuss that in detail later. It's the key to the way I make my selections. Suffice it to say that I'm not a straight "speed man" anymore. Some of my speed-loving friends argue with my methods but they can't argue with the success I've had.

Don't get me wrong. I fully appreciate the value of speed. In its place, it's wonderful. One of the best winning streaks I ever had was in 1940 at Charles Town Race Track in West Virginia. That

was a half-mile track then, and the short homestretch enabled
speed horses to win the majority of races. They had eight races
a day at Charles Town that year and I averaged four or five
winners a day. I think I won 130 of about 200 bets I placed in
that meeting.

In 1942, just before I went into the Army, I had another tremendous hot streak at Hot Springs, Arkansas. Johnny Longden
was riding there that year, and I soon recognized that he was far
superior to the other riders in the meeting. He overshadowed
them much more than it is possible for any one jockey to do
today at almost any track. I don't advocate betting on a jockey,
but I did that season with Longden, and I did nothing but win.

In 1966, 1967 and 1968 I had outstanding seasons at Atlantic
City, New Jersey. My selections in those meetings are a matter of
public record. At the request of Robert Levy, president of the
Atlantic City Race Course, I made the morning-line odds and
listed my picks for each race in the official track program. Picking
nine races a day for fifty days in all three seasons, I had winners
over 30 percent of the time. More important, a bettor who put
$2 on each of my No. 1 program selections would have come out
ahead for the meeting, which is extremely rare for a public handicapper. Of course, I didn't put my own money on all nine races a
day—betting every race every day is usually sheer financial suicide,
and I don't recommend it to anyone. I made selections for every
race because that was my job. But I bet more selectively and won
handily.

In March, 1968, on the final day of the Hialeah Park meeting,
I picked nine winners on a ten-race card. Believe me, I took home
a lot more money than I did the day I picked all seven winners
at old Bowie as a young man.

That is not to say I win all the time; nothing could be further from the truth. I've had some dandy losing streaks. My losing streaks usually start with a change of track conditions, such as when the track turns from fast to muddy. I'll admit it; I'm a failure in the mud. I really shouldn't play when the track is muddy but every once in a while I do in the hope of learning something. I have a great desire to conquer the mud, but I haven't managed it yet. When I do I think I'll take an ad in the paper to tell people about it.

Just as winning often runs in streaks, so does losing. Starting on a muddy day at Hialeah Park in 1950, I picked fifty-two consecutive losers. I broke that streak—the worst I ever had—by breaking a rule I have about never betting on horses that go off at less than even-money odds. This horse was 3–5, and I bet him because he looked "sure" and I needed something to get back to the cashiers. I put $200 on him to win.

Did he win like a 3–5 shot should? Hell no! It was life and death all the way, and at the finish line he barely stuck his nose under the wire first. Everybody around me cheered and laughed at the same time.

A couple of years after that I had a period in which I was doing so badly that nobody was laughing. My horses were being beaten by noses and heads every day. I was so low that my wife Frances and I decided to take a long rest from the track in hopes the absence would improve my luck.

As we loaded our car in Baltimore for the trip to New Jersey, a heavy rain began. Failure though I am in the mud, I knew about a horse named Barefoot Lad scheduled to run that day at Bowie, and I also knew Barefoot Lad had never lost in the mud. I also knew that he hadn't raced in the mud for several months. This meant that his recent form, established on fast tracks where he couldn't run well, would be bad and he'd likely go off at very good odds. I told Frances we'd take a detour and drive past the track. If it was still raining at race time, we'd stay to bet on Barefoot Lad.

The rain kept coming down. Barefoot Lad went off at 8–1, and the $400 I put on him (leaving about $100 for the trip home) suddenly became $3,600. Once again I was back in business. I haven't come that close to the brink since.

But right or wrong I always arrive at the track with my homework done and firm opinions on how I'm going to bet that day. If someone I know asks me which horses I like, I tell him. I'm not the kind who always looks over his shoulder when he bets because he's afraid somebody might see what he's doing. Racing is also a social game for me. I enjoy meeting people at the races and talking to them about horses. I've met some wonderful people, such as J. Edgar Hoover and his chief assistant, Clyde Tolson; Paul Richards, general manager of the Atlanta Braves; Georgie Jessel; Lorne Greene of "Bonanza" fame; John D. Shapiro, president of Laurel Race Course; and Nathan Cohen, president of the Maryland Jockey Club. I'm happy to share my choices with friends, and I've never charged a cent for my opinions.

Still, I'd much prefer that my friends had their own opinions about horses. I think they would enjoy the game more if they selected their own winners. If they work at it they will become knowledgeable and develop the ability to pick winners.

2

Phonies and Ponies

For ten cents the racing fan doesn't have to go to the trouble of doing his own handicapping. He can buy a daily newspaper and find a whole lineup of "expert" journalist handicappers who have the races all doped out. For a dollar or less he can buy what is known as a "tip sheet" at the track. That's a printed list of "winners" selected by someone who is supposed to be an even greater expert than the newspaper handicappers, probably because he charges more. In addition, all sorts of "inside" information floats around at race tracks. It supposedly comes from trainers, jockeys, grooms, exercise boys, ushers, track policemen, or others who are thought to be knowledgeable about the horses. *And* if you are really lucky you might run into a "tout," who for a fee can be persuaded to give you the "real inside."

Some of that kind of information—a very little of it—might be of use to the average bettor. The rest is worse than useless. Me, I'm death on most "tips"; I don't want any part of them. But let's examine them one at a time to see what is useful and what isn't.

All About "Tips"

Most numerous around tracks are those anonymous tips that seem to circulate of their own free will. You'll hear somebody— maybe a friend—say he's heard that such and such a trainer thinks horse so-and-so can't lose. Right then you should be suspicious. At pari-mutuel races people bet against one another, not against the track. The money that goes to the winning bettors, minus the fixed, legally set percentages that the track and state deduct for themselves, comes from the losing bettors. That means that if anyone *does* have some really good information, he's far better off keeping it to himself. If a lot of people get wind of it and bet on the tip, the odds on the horse involved will go down. The fellow who gave the original tip would win less on his bet, pro- vided he won, of course.

How do these tips start? Like this. One bettor will pick a horse for himself. When he is asked who he likes he'll name his horse. Then he'll add that he heard it from the horse's trainer. He's probably unsure of his own calculations and afraid to say,

"I figured it out myself," so he gives the credit to a supposedly knowledgeable person. The person he tells will want to believe he's heard some inside information and passes the tip along to someone else. Pretty soon dozens of people are running to the windows to bet on the horse. My advice: Completely disregard any information you can't verify.

Trainers

How about trainers? Are they really experts on picking winners? Down through the years a few trainers have had that knack. Sam Hildreth was one. He used to train for Harry F. Sinclair's Rancocas Stable, and Sinclair used to annihilate the bookmakers on the New York lawns with the information Sam Hildreth gave him. Hildreth had an uncanny "feel" for what a horse could do on a given day.

Jimmy Rowe, who used to train for the Whitneys, was another good handicapper. He had wonderful horse sense, and it would show up in the animals he raced and bred for his owners. However, Jimmy wasn't infallible. Over the years he got a reputation for turning over good stakes horses to his assistant, Freddy Hopkins. The great Equipoise was one horse he gave to Hopkins.

Ninety-nine percent of all trainers fall into one of two categories. They either think every horse they saddle will win, or they don't think any of them will. Both are all wet. Some trainers are good judges of the capabilities of their own animals, but my observation is that they usually have only the foggiest notion about the rest of the field. Don't let a trainer do your handicapping for you, even if one volunteers.

There *is* one type of information you can get from trainers that may be helpful, and that is the physical condition of their horses. If you happen to know a trainer and you're unsure about the health of one of his horses, ask him. Has the horse been training well? How is his appetite? How has he been behaving around the barn? That sort of thing. If the trainer is truthful, you'll have some useful information.

Jockeys

I put jockeys in the same two categories as trainers—optimists and pessimists. Although they may be very knowledgeable about the horses they ride, they usually don't know very much about the rest of the field. Name any great jockey, and almost invariably you'll also be naming a foolish bettor. If they ever make bookmaking legal, I'd like nothing better than to have the betting concession in the jockeys' quarters. I'd be rich in a month. Jockeys are notorious for letting their riding purses slip through their fingers.

Incidentally, it's legal for jockeys and trainers to bet, except against their own horses. It might be a good idea to forbid betting by jocks and trainers, but I'm sure the tracks wouldn't stand for it. Take away the horsemen's betting and you take away about half of a track's handle. I'm exaggerating, of course, but not by much.

As for newspaper handicappers, I'm afraid I'm not impressed with many of them. Don't get me wrong, there are some very able, conscientious handicappers who make selections and do turf writing for the papers. Russ Harris of the Miami *Herald* is one, Joe Agrella of the Chicago *Sun-Times* is another and Manny Kalish of *National Armstrong* is a third. I also think highly of Steve Klessel of the Philadelphia *Daily News* and two fellows on the *Morning Telegraph,* Teddy Cox and Gaffney, who writes under the name of "Sweep." There are others who are good, but I'm not familiar with their work.

Newspaper handicappers work with several disadvantages not of their own making. Because of the early deadlines for racing news, they must make their selections the day before the races are run. For example, they must try to select Tuesday's winners on Monday. Thus they don't have the opportunity to observe the animals on the all-important day of the race. Moreover, the newspaper handicapper's job requires that he make selections in every race, every racing day. No handicapper, no matter how expert, can have a firm, well-reasoned opinion on nine races a day, six days a week, twelve months a year. In print, all of a handicapper's winning choices look equally solid; in reality, they aren't. The fan buying the newspaper has no way of knowing which selections the handicapper really likes, and which were merely guesses. Some papers put their handicapper's "best bet" for the day in dark, bold type, but all don't follow this practice. Even when this is done, it's only a little helpful.

Too many newspapers seem more concerned with how *many* winners their handicappers pick than the winning odds. Some papers carry the selections of several handicappers. After each handicapper's name is printed the number of winners he has picked in the current meeting. That's a terrible practice because all winners aren't equal—a 2–1 shot and a 10–1 shot each count as one, but which would you rather have? I think that's why a lot of those fellows lean so heavily toward the favorites most of the time. It's easier. In recent years a number of newspapers have been keeping tabs on the financial results of their handicappers, and I think that's all to the good. However, most papers are puritanical. Apparently they don't like to admit that people go to the tracks mainly to try to win money.

Tip Sheets

The first thing a bettor without an opinion usually does when he arrives at the track is to buy one of the tip sheets. Like newspaper handicappers, some of the men who put out the tip sheets know what they are doing and some don't. A lot of horseplayers sense this, but they buy three or four sheets anyway to find the races all agree on. Buying a lot of sheets is the surest way to get mixed up. The one or two horses on which they all agree will be outstanding choices that go off at something like 3–5. You don't need a sheet to find that kind of horse, even if you wanted to put up $5 to win $3.

Ronnie Schroeder, who goes under the name of Clocker Lawton, has made a tremendous success with his orange sheet, which is sold in tracks all over the East. I know Ronnie fairly well. He started as a newsboy at Pimlico in Maryland, where he sold Jack's Green Card, which was put out by Buzzy Appleton, who is now dead.

Even as a newsboy Ronnie was a $10 or $20 bettor and a good, hard worker with the racing charts. Through his own efforts he became a good handicapper. When he thought he could pick more winners than Buzzy he went off on his own. I think Ronnie is better than Buzzy ever was. His style of selecting winners is fairly close to mine, and our choices will often coincide in three or four races a day. Ronnie has an organization that works for him now while he stays mostly in New York. Thus I think that during summer his card is better at the New York tracks than it is at the others.

Jack's Green Card has also been successful over the years, but I don't know the men who run it today. The rest of the cards? I don't like to say too much about them. Some may have good meetings at one track or another. Sometimes it will pay to look at a "hot" card. As a rule, though, beware of tip sheets' claims to expertness. The guy at the track shouting about the 20–1 winner his card picked never mentions the thirty or forty 20–1 shots of his that finished someplace in Asia.

One trouble with all the tip sheets, as well as with the newspaper handicappers, is that they tell you what to bet, but not how. A lot of bettors become frustrated at this. They bet a professional handicapper's top selection in one race, and his second choice will win. Then they bet his second or third choice and the No. 1 pick will be right. If I played with one of those tip sheets and I felt I had to bet every race, I'd take the longest shot of the top three selections in each race and bet it. Working that way, I'd have fewer winners than if I bet all the Number 1 picks, but I'd probably lose less money.

For some reason tip sheets seem to have more success with Daily Doubles than with other races. I rarely bet the Double or other parlays of that sort, because, in my opinion, they're gimmicks to separate the $2 bettor from his money. But if you must play the Double and you don't learn to develop opinions of your own even after reading this book, I suggest you follow this procedure. Take a card or a newspaper handicapper you trust and "box" the top three selections in the first and second races; that is, buy tickets on 1–1, 1–2 and 1–3, 2–1, 2–2, 2–3, and 3–1, 3–2, 3–3. You'll have nine combinations, and a $2 bet on each will cost you $18. Maybe you Daily Double players will lose a little less that way by winning a few.

What About Touts?

Touts are another matter entirely. Their stock-in-trade is larceny, not information. My advice is to stay away from them completely, otherwise you'll only come to grief. I learned this very early in my racing education, again through the bad example set by my father's horseplaying.

In the 1920s the *Morning Telegraph* used to be full of tout ads. They read something like this: "Send me $10 and I'll send you a winner." The *Telegraph* stopped carrying those ads about thirty years ago when it became a higher-class publication.

I remember an ad for a tout named Harvey Ames. He was a classy tout and advertised a winner for $100 or your money back. My dad, who was competent in his own business, would listen to anybody when it came to horse racing, so he sent Harvey Ames the $100 and immediately received a wire giving him a horse in a certain race. He placed the bet and the horse lost. Dad wired Ames to return the $100. "Oh no!" answered Ames. "I promised you a winner—not a winner the first time." He sent the name of another horse. That horse also lost. Finally, on the third try, Harvey Ames sent Dad a winner. The horse was 7–10, paying $3.40 for $2. But Dad had lost two bets, so he was down the drain even with Ames' winner. As touts go, though, Ames was honest. At least he delivered a winner as promised.

Touts flourish, I think, because of the larceny in the hearts of so many horseplayers (not unlike many people who don't play the horses). They want to get something for nothing. They enjoy the thrill of what seems to be a shady deal. You will see this streak of larceny in people who wouldn't think of doing a dishonest thing in their regular professions or jobs.

The late Al Jolson was like that. In my book he was the greatest entertainer who ever lived. Jolson was a racing fan and a big bettor. But Jolson would bet on stories, not on horses. He was a sucker for every tout on the track. The more involved the tale, the better Jolson liked it.

One of Jolson's favorite characters was a steeplechase rider named Fennessey, who was a tout on the side. One summer while

Jolson was appearing in a Broadway show, Fennessey was riding a steeplechase mount he thought was fit and ready for a big win. Fennessey decided that this was a good opportunity to get a big bet from Jolson. Did Fennessey simply go to Jolson and tell him he was riding a horse he thought was in condition to win? No, sir! Fennessey gave Jolson the larceny bit. He told him he hadn't been letting the horse run before but that this time he would and that for a couple of hundred dollars he'd pay off a few other jockeys to make the race a sure thing. According to the story, Al is supposed to have gone for it and given Fennessey the money for the other jockeys, which, of course, went right into Fennessey's pocket. He also bet $1,000 for Fennessey in addition to the much larger sum he bet for himself.

The race unfolded. It was a two-mile steeplechase and Fennessey's mount started off right behind another horse. That was the way it went. Fennessey was second after a mile, second after 1½ miles, second at the last jump and second past the tape by a neck, even though he was banging his horse against the other one every chance he got. So the bet was gone, right? Wrong. Fennessey didn't have anything to lose, so he took a chance and claimed a foul. Lo and behold, the stewards disqualified the winner and gave the race to Fennessey. Jolson won his bet.

Fennessey dressed and ran downstairs to find Jolson and collect his share. Jolson was all smiles, having just won a bundle. He congratulated Fennessey and told him he'd done a great job fixing all those other riders. "There's only one thing I don't understand," Jolson is supposed to have said. "How did you fix those stewards to give you the race on a foul?"

But when it came to sheer artistry among touts, Fennessey couldn't hold a candle to Tommy (The Maestro) Francis and Mose Shapoff. I knew both of them very well.

Tommy Francis was born in the same town in Italy as Enrico Caruso. They called him The Maestro because he'd studied the violin. He and Caruso came to the United States at about the same time. Caruso went to the opera and Tommy went to the track. After Caruso became a big success he was one of Tommy's best customers. At his peak, Tommy was a pretty fair handicapper. He also had a convincing manner, a lot of braggadocio and a taste for good living. Whenever he won a bet or collected a big touting fee he'd give an elaborate dinner for all his friends at the old Villanova restaurant in New York.

Like all touts, Tommy usually talked only about his wins. One of the few stories he told about a loser involved Caruso. Caruso was very sick at the time, practically on his deathbed. Tommy had a horse at Belmont Park that day which, according to his figures, was a winner even before the race was run. He had to tell Caruso about this horse and get a bet from him.

When Tommy appeared at Caruso's apartment the butler asked him to leave because Caruso was ill, but Tommy wouldn't take no for an answer. He started yelling and making a ruckus in the hall until Caruso heard it and told the butler to let him in.

Caruso listened to Tommy's story and shook his head sadly. "Tommy," he said, "the doctors tell me I haven't long to live. What am I going to gain even if this horse wins?"

Tommy was ready with an answer. "You want to go out a winner, don't you?"

Caruso bet $500 on the horse and gave Tommy something to bet for himself. Tommy, like an honest tout, went out and bet the money. This time he was really right. With $\frac{1}{16}$ of a mile to go, his horse was ahead by six lengths and there seemed to be no way he could lose. But strange are the happenings at race tracks. Moments before the finish the horse jumped over the fence and out of the race. Caruso died soon after that and Tommy went into a long losing streak. Being superstitious, Tommy insisted that when the horse jumped the fence, it was a sign that the Devil was after him.

The champion of them all, though, was Mose Shapoff, a life-long friend. Mose was round and florid-faced and a great story-teller. He could tout a wooden Indian.

Once in Louisville, Kentucky, Mose heard about a wealthy merchant who loved to bet but only when he'd received information from jockeys. This was too much for Mose to pass up. It was a challenge to him to tout this man.

The merchant's favorite rider was Sonny Workman, one of the best jockeys of the 1930s. It was Kentucky Derby week and Workman was slated to ride several very good horses. Mose thought this would be the perfect time to get some bets.

Mose was thinking and thinking about this—what a mind he had!—when suddenly he saw a little character at the·track called Jakey the Burglar. Jakey, an exercise boy, was built like Work-man and bore a great facial resemblance to him. Right away it flashed into Mose's mind to sell Jakey to the man as Workman. Jakey, who fully deserved his nickname, went along with the scheme for a share of the action.

Mose dressed Jakey up, brought him to the rich man's office and introduced him as Workman. The man was so thrilled and enthusiastic that Mose couldn't stop at mere touting. He said to the man, "Not only are we going to give you winners this morn-ing, but Sonny, here, likes you and wants to work for you. I'll sell you his contract if you'll buy some horses." He added ex-pansively: "I'll help you buy the horses and train them for you. I'll even be your partner."

The man readily agreed and told Mose he'd meet him after the day's races to work out the details.

That afternoon the man went to the track with the tips on the two Workman horses Mose had given him. Both were very good horses, and the fellow won both of his bets. He was so happy he took it on himself to go down to visit Workman in the paddock after the second winner.

"Hi, Sonny," he said. "Those were a couple of great races you rode today."

Workman said thanks but, of course, gave no indication that he recognized the guy.

The man said, "Don't you recognize me? You were in my office this morning. I'm going to buy your contract once I've started my own stable."

Workman said, "What's the matter with you? Are you crazy? I never saw you before. Get out of here."

Naturally this made the man suspicious, but he'd won two good bets and he still was happy. He went to pay Mose for the tips and told him about seeing Workman and how funny the jockey had acted.

"Sonny acts that way sometimes," said Mose, thinking fast. "He might not want to go through with the deal."

Mose promised the man that after they went into partnership to buy the horses, he'd talk to Workman again.

But who showed up right then? Jakey the Burglar. "You got the sucker's money yet?" he shouted to Mose, not seeing the man. The jig was up for Mose and Jakey.

I hope such stories will convince you to stay clear of touts. I'd like to give you one more piece of advice. Never, never give your money to a stranger to bet for you. One friend of mine learned that the hard way by dealing with Jakey the Burglar.

One racing season in New England, Jakey met a man who wanted to make a fast buck at the track. Jakey obliged by cooking up stories about fixed races. His plan, typical for a tout, was to take part of the winnings, if by chance the fellow should win, and come up with an excuse if he lost. That's the way touts operate.

Jakey and his sucker went to the track together, and the man, who was really green, gave Jakey his money to bet. This was wonderful for Jakey. He'd originally planned to give the guy some horses that had a chance of winning. Now he switched tactics. He picked a longshot going off at 8–1, took the $500 bet and put it right in his pocket after pretending to bet. Wouldn't you know it! The horse won and Jakey owed his client $4,000.

When the sucker asked for his money, Jakey said, "No, we're not going to settle for a lousy $4,000. We'll put it all on the next race and really make a killing." The man didn't want to do it, but he was impressed with Jakey because of the first·winner and agreed to let the money ride. Jakey picked an even more impossible longshot this time—a horse going off at 15–1. Off Jakey went to pretend to bet. Again the impossible horse won, and now Jakey was in real trouble; he owed the guy $60,000.

This time Jakey practically had to wrestle with the guy, but he finally convinced him that he would triple his money in the last race with a horse named Brass Monkey, a great New England favorite because of the way he would charge from behind in the last quarter-mile. Sometimes he'd win and sometimes he'd lose, but he always put on a good show.

Brass Monkey, at 2–1, had a reasonable chance of winning, so the sucker went along with Jakey again. The horse ran his usual race, coming from dead last, and won by a nose. The minute

Brass Monkey crossed the wire, Jakey the Burglar was out the gate and was never heard from again.

3

99 44/100% Pure

The lure of larceny in racing doesn't end with the touts and tipsters. Joe Palmer, the late racing writer for the old New York *Herald Tribune,* once wrote that if a track were to advertise that on a certain day a race would be fixed for an unnamed horse to win, people would break down the gates trying to get in and bet. Every horse in the race would be played, and every bettor would be absolutely sure he was right. Such is the larceny in the minds of many, many people who bet on the horses.

I've been around racing long enough to know that it isn't 100 percent on the level, but then, no business is. A few people will always be looking for an edge—a way to make a dishonest dollar. Nevertheless, I will match the honesty and integrity of the people who own, train and ride race horses with that of any group. In my judgment, the game is 99 44/100% pure.

Imputations of dishonesty circulate around race tracks in much the same manner as baseless "tips" on horses. A player who loses a bet will immediately look for a scapegoat. He will say that the jockey "pulled" his horse—wouldn't let him run—or that the horse's trainer loaded him up with so much hay and water before the race that he couldn't run properly. The "logic" behind this argument is that the next time the horse runs he will go off at higher odds and the jockey or trainer will be in a position to cash a big bet. In the vast majority of cases the man who starts such a rumor has nothing to base it on. He is merely working off his anger at being wrong in his betting.

Betting on horses is far too complex a matter to allow suspicions of larceny to enter into your calculations. It's tough enough to weigh properly all the legitimate factors that go into selecting a winner without adding the alleged motives of the men who train and ride the horses. Once you start trying to figure out who is honest and who isn't, you are lost before you begin. If for some reason you are convinced that racing isn't on the level, you'd better stay home. Trainers and jockeys make mistakes in judgment while handling horses, just as business and professional men do in their fields. Close observation at the track will alert you to which of these people are competent and which are not. Yet in trying to handicap a particular race, you must assume that every horse is out there to win. There is no other way to approach the game.

How You Are Protected

Racing has gone to great lengths to police itself. The Thorough-bred Racing Protective Bureau (TRPB), an interstate investigatory force formed by the tracks in 1945, keeps a close watch on all facets of the game. Films or videotapes taken of each race at just about every track in the country have gone a long way toward helping stewards to pinpoint and punish fouls and other irregularities that can affect a race's outcome.

Modern chemistry can detect substances given to horses to make them run faster. I don't always agree with the way such tests are administered by racing officials. In the 1968 Kentucky Derby, for instance, Dancer's Image was disqualified as the winner because Butazolidin, a painkiller, was found in his urine after the race, and the purse was given to Forward Pass, who wasn't even tested. Still, the use of such tests can be a great safeguard for the public.

Lip tattoos and other means of identifying horses have virtually eliminated "ringers" from the races. A ringer is a horse that is substituted for a slower horse without the public's knowledge. In past decades this was a great problem for the game. Still, attempts at larceny persist, as I can testify at first hand. In the main, they stem from ignorance.

Some Personal Experiences

In the summer of 1937, when I was managing the Paragon Stable, we were campaigning at the New England tracks with great success. As I've said, Bold Turk won a number of New England stakes races that year. Other horses in our stable were winning many cheaper races. However, like all stables, we had two or three horses that weren't winning. This bothered the owner, Mr. Silberman, greatly.

One day at Suffolk Downs I received a call from Silberman in New York. He was very excited because he'd found the way Hirsch Jacobs' horses were winning just about every race they entered in New York that season.

"Did you know Hirsch Jacobs was a pigeon fancier when he was a kid on the East Side of New York?" Silberman said. "Well, I got it from a very good source that he has something called pigeon milk that he gives to all his horses. It gives them great energy. I bought some of the stuff from a trainer who's a good friend of his. I'm sending you some by truck."

At that time I knew Hirsch Jacobs only by reputation. In the years since we have become friends, but even then from what I'd heard about Hirsch I was convinced that he was a completely honest man, one who well deserved his title as the best young trainer in the country. He didn't need any magic "hop"—stimulant—to make his horses win. He did it with his skill. In the years that followed he proved his worth beyond a shadow of a doubt. In eleven of the twelve years from 1933 through 1944, he saddled more winners than any other U.S. trainer.

When Silberman mentioned pigeon milk to me, I hit the ceiling. "How much did you pay for it?" I asked. He said he'd paid $5,000. I asked where he got it and he mentioned a trainer whose reputation for honesty was less than perfect. I told him he'd been robbed, but he wouldn't believe it. He insisted I use the stuff.

One of our unsuccessful horses was Muggins, a filly I'd claimed the previous winter at Hialeah Park for $7,500. She was a bad claim. She couldn't win for $7,500, $6,000 or even $5,000. It just so happened that the next week I entered her in a $2,000 claiming race I felt certain she could win. Silberman told me to use the pigeon milk on Muggins before her next start. I was pretty disgusted by this time, so in order to get him off my back I said I would.

A few days later a truck pulled up at our barn and a dozen or so gallon jugs of a white liquid were unloaded. I opened one and tried some. It tasted like weak, sweet milk. Naturally, I didn't want bottles of suspicious-looking liquids that I couldn't explain around my barn, so I immediately sent one to a chemist to be tested. The results indicated it was ordinary cow's milk, water and sugar.

I made up my mind to teach Mr. Silberman a lesson. He phoned me almost every day that week and asked one question: "Are you giving Muggins the pigeon milk?"

Each time I told him, "Yes."

The race was run and Silberman placed a big bet on Muggins. She went off at very low odds, almost even-money, and because of the great drop in class she won easily. Silberman was very happy with his winnings and was all smiles. "See," he told me. "You thought I was nuts buying that pigeon milk. You were wrong."

Back at the barn I showed him all the unopened jugs of pigeon milk. I explained that Muggins won because she was in a cheap $2,000 claiming race (incidentally, she was claimed in that race). I showed him the chemist's report. "Take your pigeon's milk home and drink it," I said. "Maybe it will make you fly."

I suppose that might be considered a funny story. But here's one that's not so funny. It cost me my stable agent's license in New Jersey for a year, and it nearly meant the end of me in racing.

Some of the People You Meet Around Tracks

To preface the story, I ought to point out that you meet all sorts of people around the tracks. Racing is a public game—just about anyone can enter the track and bet—and it is natural to strike up conversations about the sport with people you hardly know. I've met many fine people in this way. I've also met a few who weren't so fine. Three of the latter were Joe Adonis, Salvatore Morretti and his brother Willie. Senator Kefauver's investigations in the early 1950s revealed all three to be gangsters or to have close ties with gangsters.

I'd known Sally Morretti slightly when I was young. He was in the textile business near Paterson, and from time to time he would buy machinery from my father. I later got to know him better at the tracks, where he was a horse-owner, trainer and bettor. My dealings with him were limited strictly to racing. In the late 1940s I bought and managed a horse named Gigolo for him. Gigolo was a fine animal and twice broke track records at the old Havre de Grace track in Maryland. There was no mystery about my handling that horse for Sally Morretti. He was the registered owner and I was on record as his agent. Through Sally I met his brother Willie.

I met Joe Adonis at the tracks after World War II. He had heard of my reputation for picking winners, and one day at Monmouth Park he sought my advice on a race. A friend of his, the trainer Albert (Spec) Dunne, had a horse named Glen Heather running. One of my horses, Happy Task, was in the same race. Adonis, a tall and handsome man with sleek black hair (he got the name "Adonis" from a chorus girl), introduced himself to me and asked what I thought of the race. I told him I didn't think Glen Heather had a chance to win against my horse. He thanked me and then bet on Glen Heather. Happy Task won. After that he sought me out more frequently.

Adonis and I became fairly friendly. I like Italian food, so we had several meals together at a good Italian restaurant he knew in Brooklyn. As far as I knew, his business was running a car-hauling service in New Jersey. Of course, I'd heard people say other things about him, and about Sally and Willie Morretti too. But if you believed everything you heard about people who frequent race tracks, you'd never talk to anyone. I believed that Adonis and the Morrettis were legitimate businessmen who liked to bet on horses—period. I stopped associating with all three as quickly as I could when the Kefauver investigations revealed them to be underworld figures. Maybe I was wrong in taking people at face value, but that was my only "crime." But that wasn't the way the New Jersey Racing Commission saw it. In 1951, after Senator Kefauver launched his hearings into racketeering, the TRPB began a series of investigations of its own on the racing activities of gangland figures. In 1951, when I applied for a renewal of my agent's license in New Jersey in connection with my employment with the Carolyn-K Stable, I was turned down. The reason: "Associating with undesirables."

I Get Investigated

The news hit me like a bomb. I had told the TRPB the truth about my contacts with Adonis and the Morrettis. I couldn't imagine how they could make anything sinister out of that, but I found out when I saw the report the TRPB had filed with the New Jersey racing commissioners. The TRPB had talked to many people at the tracks who, for one reason or another, didn't care for me and picked up some very wild accusations. Without any further investigation they presented these accusations as "facts" in their report. In racing you are guilty until proved innocent. I was refused a license, and it was my job to show that the report was false, but I couldn't even obtain a formal copy of the charges against me. Fortunately, a good friend who was high up in racing gave me a copy. This helped greatly in my defense.

I do not doubt the motives of the TRPB in investigating me. I am sure they had the best interests of the game at heart. But I do quarrel strongly with their methods. The report was aggressively accusatory in tone and insinuative in language. My wife was described as "believed to be the wife of the subject." How do you like that? I would have showed them our marriage certificate in a minute if they'd asked.

In another section of the report they said I had a record of six arrests by the Paterson, N.J., police department, "all for motor vehicle and disorderly conduct violations." That sounds pretty bad, doesn't it, especially the part about "violations." The truth is that I'd had five traffic tickets in Paterson and one "disorderly conduct" arrest. When I was thirteen years old I was arrested with a bunch of other kids for fooling around in a railroad freight yard. The railroad detective took us in and we were booked by the police. We were released immediately to our parents, but it went into the records as an arrest just the same.

The report made a big thing out of my June, 1950, arrest in Clifton, N.J., in connection with a raid on a bookie joint. It mentioned that I was acquitted of all charges, but only in passing. Instead it dealt mostly with some unsavory people whom I didn't know but who were arrested in the same raid. The point they tried to make was that if I was in the place with those characters, I was one of them.

The real story was simple, but it wasn't presented in the TRPB report. The previous winter in Florida I'd been visited by an old friend from Paterson. In the course of the visit I'd loaned him $500. When I got back to New Jersey that June, I phoned him about the debt. He told me to meet him at a certain time and gave me an address. When I got to the address, the man who answered the door told me my friend would be along soon and that he had asked me to wait for him. The place looked like someone's home, and I sat alone waiting in a downstairs room. The police came in shortly afterward and arrested me and some others who were in upstairs rooms. They found some betting slips upstairs, and two of the men were later convicted of bookmaking. As I said, I was acquitted in court.

There were other allegations. The report quoted two jockeys who complained that I had attempted to "dictate" a choice of other riders to the owners they worked for. Both were incompetent jockeys in my opinion. I'd never allowed them to ride any of my horses, and I suppose that was their way of getting back at me. On one occasion an owner who employed one of those jocks had asked me for my opinion about the boy, and I'd told him I thought he'd do better with another rider. That was the full extent of it. It's certainly no crime to express an opinion.

There was a charge—totally untrue—that I had "attempted to have a rider finish second" with a horse in Florida. The man who told the TRPB this admitted he wasn't able to provide any particulars, and the TRPB apparently didn't check it out further. But there it was in the report.

From the tone of the report, the aim of the TRPB was to show I was a "front" who raced, in my own or my wife's name, horses that were really owned by gangsters. The "evidence" for this was the record of a phone call I had made to Joe Adonis from a Baltimore hotel. No mention of the content of the call was given in the report. Actually, I had made that call to return one of his. He was asking for my opinion about a certain race. I gave it to him just as I give my opinions to others.

To show how baseless the "front man" accusation was, in another section of the same report the TRPB quoted a man who said he'd "heard" I had borrowed money to claim a horse, a practice frowned upon by racing authorities. It was untrue, but consider it in context: If rich gangsters were giving me money to buy horses for them, why would I be going around looking for loans for the same purpose? The incongruity of it apparently didn't occur to the TRPB.

It took more than a year before I could arrange a hearing to prove my innocence. In the interim I wasn't allowed to race my own horses or manage those of the Carolyn-K Stable. It was a tough year.

I was exonerated at the hearing, although I wasn't accused of any crime and it was strictly an administrative matter for the New Jersey Racing Commission.

Under questioning by Benjamin Taub, a deputy state's attorney-general, and my own lawyer, I fully explained every charge brought against me. I knew I had convinced the commissioners of my innocence about midway through the proceedings, after I had explained the real nature of my acquaintance with Joe Adonis. I had said that I'd never received money from Adonis or anyone else for my opinions on the horses. Mr. Taub sought to trip me up on this.

"Mr. Lewin," he said, "did anyone else ever call you up and ask for similar information?"

I answered, "Yes."

"Who?" he asked, leaning forward in anticipation.

"J. Edgar Hoover, for one," I answered.

That hearing also was gratifying to me because of the way so many of my friends spoke out in my support. Colonel Isidore Bieber, Hirsch Jacobs' partner in racing and breeding horses (the Bieber-Jacobs Stable led the nation's breeders in 1967), wrote a letter to the commission on my behalf. So did Charles McLennon, who was then racing secretary at Laurel Race Course, and Dr. Leon Levy, a horse-owner, major stockholder in the Atlantic City race track and one of the finest men in racing. A delegation from the Horsemen's Benevolent & Protective Association, an organization of owners, appeared and delivered a statement attesting to my good reputation. Mr. Kirschbaum also appeared and spoke. Others would have appeared, but I told them I didn't think it would be necessary. From that day to this, my qualifications as an owner and agent have never again been questioned.

What About Larceny?

Let's move on now to larceny at the races. For my money, by far the most overplayed subject is the "fixed" race. Ninety-nine out of a hundred people think races are fixed "to make a longshot win." What's more, they think race-fixing is an easy matter, something that can be cooked up on short order with no one the wiser. Both assumptions are far from the truth.

The fact is that fixing a race is extremely difficult because horses don't necessarily run the way you'd like them to. Several years ago at Saratoga they were making a movie on the life of Man O' War. One scene called for a re-enactment of the 1919 race when Man O' War suffered the only loss of his 21-race career, appropriately enough to a horse named Upset. They had to run that scene about a dozen times because one of the horses, who wasn't supposed to be the winner, kept winning. It took several days of pulling and hauling by the jockeys before the horses finished in the order called for by the script.

That's the way it has worked in real races, too. Back in 1935 at Rockingham Park, a guy set about to try to rig a race. The way I heard it, the race was a cheap $1,500 claimer. The field was a small one, seven horses in all, and the worst of them was trained by Lew Williams. Lew's horse was a 20–1 shot that deserved to be 20–1.

Lew got wind of the fact that the fixer was paying jocks and trainers $100 apiece to pull their horses. Lew wanted his $100, so he went up to the fixer in the track kitchen the morning of the race and said, "How come you left my horse out of the deal? He has a good chance to win."

The fixer laughed and told Lew his horse wasn't going to be anywhere near the front at the finish line and didn't give him the money.

You know how the race ended—Lew's horse won. The other jockeys got so tangled up trying to make the fixer's horse win that nobody else ran at all. It was the easiest win in poor Lew's life.

Fix a race to make a longshot win? That's ridiculous. It would upset the running of the race to such a degree that half the people in the grandstand would know things weren't right; and the stewards would know it too. I assure you I've never been involved in tampering with a race. But logic tells me a "real" fix, if there is one, would work something like this: The race would be one in which only two horses figured to have a chance to win. The people interested in fixing the race would try to stop one of those two horses. Both horses would be favored by the public in the betting on the basis of their form, so neither would go off at long odds. Maybe one would be 8–5, the other 5–2. An 8–5 shot represents about 38 percent of the mutuel win pool, and a 5–2 shot about 29 percent. That adds up to 67 per cent of the race in the fixer's pocket if his moves are successful. That is a very good gambler's chance.

Would the fixer bet extremely heavily on the fixed race? No. Even if he placed his bets with several bookies, very heavy betting would probably alert the bookies that something was foul and they'd probably dump those bets right back onto the track so that the odds on the fixer's horse would drop. The fixer would bet, of course, but not so heavily as to arouse suspicion. If the fixer did any betting at all at the track, it would be on a "stiff" in the race, a horse with very little chance of winning. A big bet, say $1,000, might pull enough odds-board watchers with it to give him a better price on his real horse. Remember, all this is mere conjecture on my part. But if you even have reason to believe a race is being tampered with, lay off. Chances are it will be set up to make you guess wrong.

Other forms of racing larceny deal with the buying and selling of horses. A master of the art was Colonel Phil Chinn, a profane, heavy-drinking horse-breeder. Chinn had a couple of tricks. On his breeding farm he had a track where he worked his horses. The track had movable distance poles. If Chinn wanted to sell a horse to a sucker, he'd move one of the poles closer to the finish line than it should have been. When the man clocked the horse Chinn was trying to sell, it would register a far faster time than it really could run because it was running a shorter distance.

Another trick of the late Mr. Chinn had to do with horseshoes. He'd work out a horse wearing heavy shoes on a public track so it would post slow clockings. Then he would approach a buyer and tell him the horse had improved vastly. When the buyer wanted proof of this "improvement," off would come the heavy shoes and down would come the horse's time.

Fatty Anderson and I bought many horses from the good colonel. We weren't taken in by his larceny, of course. Chinn often had some really good horses to sell, but he tried to sell them for two to three times their worth. When he couldn't get his price and came down to earth, I would buy.

There's another horse-selling gimmick I like to call the "fatted calf" ploy. Some breeders, before they put their yearlings up for an auction sale, fatten them up on feed and molasses. They oil their coats to a bright shine and show them off under skillfully placed lights. This makes a horse look like a peach. A lot of people have bought fat, sleek horses in yearling sales and found themselves with nanny goats after training them for a week. Those nanny goats, however, still may be able to run.

I guess that sort of thing should be called "legal larceny," and it's certainly not limited to horse racing. Anyone with a product to sell will try to dress it up to look its best. I also think that taking full advantage of the rules of racing comes under this category.

Often, after a race has been run, the INQUIRY sign is flashed on the results board. This means that the stewards, who supervise the running of each race, are looking into a possible irregularity in its running. In the majority of cases the inquiry will involve a claim of foul by one rider against another. The two main types of fouls that occur during a race are "herding," where the rider of one contending horse will force another horse to the outside of the track, and "crowding," where a rider will try to squeeze a horse that's challenging him into the rail. If the stewards decide that the rider of one of the top three in a race is guilty, his horse will be dropped in the order of finish or disqualified outright. For rough riding, the jockey usually faces suspension.

There's another rule in racing that says that a horse must maintain a fairly straight course down the homestretch. To be applied, however, the infraction must affect the outcome of a race, which often makes the decision a difficult one for the stewards. I've used this rule to my advantage, and I've had it used against me.

One day in June, 1939, at Suffolk Downs, a big wind whipped up suddenly and blew off part of the top of the grandstand. The trainer Phil Bieber, Colonel Isidore Bieber's brother, got some splinters in his leg in the mishap and was taken to the hospital. As a favor to him, I ran his stable while he was recuperating. He had a horse named Dreel, who was too old for racing—eight but a fair sprinter. I put him in the second race at Rockingham the next week, a cheap ¾-mile claimer, which I thought he could win.

It rained that day—the track was a sea of slop. I'm not much of a Daily Double player, but in the first race was Tow Rope, who usually wasn't very good but could run like crazy in the mud. Tow Rope was 7–1, so I bought fifty $2 Daily Double tickets on Tow Rope and Dreel.

Tow Rope won the first race easily, and when the Double payments were flashed I saw that I stood to get $80 for each of my $2 tickets, or $4,000 in all, if Dreel won. Dreel went off at 9–10, and I really rooted for him. But things didn't go well for Dreel. Against him was Fair Time, another good mudder. Fair Time, a 3–1 shot, took a 5-length early lead, with Dreel second and the rest of the field far behind. Fair Time maintained that lead into the homestretch. Once he got to the stretch, however, he started going very, very wide, seeking firmer ground. My horse closed somewhat, but Fair Time still won with room to spare.

Then I remembered the rule about horses maintaining straight courses, so I took a chance and claimed a foul against Fair Time. My jockey in that race, Ruperto Donoso, didn't speak English very well, so I yelled my foul claim up to Tom Thorpe, the state steward in New Hampshire, and sent Donoso up to make it official.

Tom Thorpe was an honest, conscientious man, but, I believed, he had a quirk—he loved to see favorites win. Dreel was favored over Fair Time, so that could be in my favor; that and the rule. The stewards conferred for about 10 minutes before taking down Fair Time as the winner and putting up Dreel. Tom Thorpe was bothered about that decision, and later that night at dinner I assured him he had done the right thing. The letter of the law was in my favor, but actually I think I stole that one—legal larceny.

But those things come back to haunt you. Several years ago

I ran Local Gossip at Laurel in Maryland. The race was a mile over the turf course, he was 8–1, and he won by 3½ lengths. He bore out in the stretch, but that didn't bother me. I was busy patting myself on the back and rushing off to cash my winning tickets when I saw INQUIRY flash on the board. I stopped in my tracks. Oh oh! I thought, I'm getting paid back for Dreel. And that was the way it turned out, despite all my arguing.

Legal Larceny

Fatty Anderson used the phrase "legal larceny" in connection with his practice of running claiming horses for half of what they were worth, but you don't see much of that today. The public is too smart. If you get a reputation for that sort of thing, your horses will go off at odds of 1–2 or thereabouts. That doesn't make it worth the betting risk, especially when you add the risk of having your horse claimed. I used Fatty's method with my own horses for a few years until the time came when other owners wouldn't let me keep a horse. They claimed everything I ran.

Perhaps the most prevalent form of legal larceny on the tracks these days comes in the writing of the conditions for races. Each track has a racing secretary who writes the "condition book," lines up horses for each day's races and assigns weights in handicap events. Sometimes, a race will be "written" for a horse; that is, the conditions will be set in such a way as to give one horse an extremely good shot at winning. Usually the beneficiary will be an owner or trainer who has run a lot of horses at a meeting without much luck; the racing secretary will be trying to do him a favor. There's nothing especially wrong with this practice. It is done right out in the open where anyone who can read will see it. But many people neglect to read the conditions of the races and thus miss some good bets.

For example, a race was run during a recent spring season at one of the Eastern tracks. The conditions read like this:

1 1/16 MILES
Allowances. Purse $7,500. Fillies and mares. 4-year-olds and upward which have not won $2,650 twice over a mile since Oct. 15 other than maiden, claiming, optional or starter. Weight, 121 lbs. Non-winners of $4,875 at a mile or over since March 15 allowed 3 lbs., $3,905 at a mile or over since Nov. 18, 6 lbs., $3,300 at a mile or over since Oct. 14, 9 lbs.

Anyone reading the past-performance charts of the horses in that race knew that the key words in the conditions were "at a mile or over." There was a filly in the race fresh from several impressive triumphs at distances of slightly less than a mile. Her last mile victory had come the previous summer, well in advance of the Oct. 14 cutoff date, so she received the full 9-pound weight allowance.

Naturally the filly went off as the favorite in the race; her odds were just above even-money. Horses don't always win races "written" for them, but she did, and by 10 lengths. That's about the way I'd figured her to win, so I risked a few dollars despite the low odds. If everybody at the track that day had read the conditions of the race carefully, she'd have gone off at odds of 1–2.

Did I say 99 44/100% pure? Make that 99 43/100%.

4

Pace Makes the Race

I've said before that picking winners at the race track is no easy matter, and I think it's worth repeating. Handicapping is an art. It has never been a science, nor do I believe it ever will be. In the pages to follow, I will list and discuss the various factors that come into play at the track. I am methodical in my horse-playing and there are some general guidelines which I follow and which I will give you, but I do *not* have what is known as a "system." I don't think that anything as complex as horse racing can be broken down into simple rules that will fit all or even most circumstances. Recently, I saw a book billed as containing 100 "systems" for betting on the horses. Now, I ask you, if just one of those 100 "systems" really worked, why would you need the other 99?

Systems?

There are a few garden-variety systems which a surprisingly large number of racing fans use. One involves adding the morning-line odds to the weights carried by horses in each race, and betting on the horse with the lowest total. Another simply recommends betting on the horse with the second-lowest final odds in each race.

Would you like to know a far-out theory? It's called the "Holy Ghost" system. When a jockey or post position wins twice in the first four races on a nine-race card, you're supposed to keep playing that jockey or post position because it is "sure" to win a third time and thus complete a "trinity." Besides being blasphemous, it's the stupidest thing I've ever heard. Yet I've seen people use it.

The theories about betting second-favorites and adding morning-line odds to weights contain germs of truth. If a novice bettor sticks to either system, he'll probably lose less in the long run. Unfortunately, the long run never comes for most people. Equally important, it's not much fun to bet with some simple, pat system. The challenge of handicapping is an intellectual one in which you match your knowledge and judgment against those of everyone else at the track. To me, that is the excitement and appeal of the game. The information I give you should help you form your own opinions about the horses. After that, it's up to you.

Good handicapping requires prerace study. Before going to the track, buy a copy of either the *Morning Telegraph* or the *Daily Racing Form* as early as possible. They contain the complete results of the previous day's thoroughbred races and the past performances of the horses scheduled to run that day. Both papers are published by Triangle Publications, Inc.

If you've never used either newspaper, free booklets that explain the many symbols and abbreviations they use are available at newsstands at any race track. The *Morning Telegraph* past-performance chart—presented here for brief illustrative purposes —is for the horse Full Reach as he went into a ¾-mile allowance race for three-year-olds on June 10, 1968, at Delaware Park.

On the top line, opposite Full Reach's name, are the letters "B. g," which means that Full Reach is a brown (B) gelding (g)—a gelding is a desexed male. After that comes the year of his birth, 1965, and his birthplace, Maryland (Md.). "By Cyane-Pink Rosay, by Rosemont" means that his sire (father) was Cyane, his mother was Pink Rosay and her sire was Rosemont. Below that is listed Full Reach's owner (Christiana Stable), his trainer (H. S. Clark) and his breeder, also Christiana Stable.

The boldface number, 113, on the top line is the weight Full Reach is assigned to carry in the day's race. The weight total includes the weight of his rider, saddle and gear. To the right of Full Reach's weight assignment is his past-performance summary for the last two years. After 1968 are the numbers 4, 1, 0, 0. That means he started four times in 1968, finished first once and didn't finish second or third in his other races. The final figure, $2,760, indicates his winnings for the year. The *0* in the 1967 column means he didn't race that year.

The top line of the chart itself begins with the date of Full Reach's last race—June 3, 1968. "3Del" means that the race was the third at Delaware Park that day. "Fst" means that the track

Full Reach B.g., (1965-Md), by Cyane-Pink Rosay, by Rosemont

Christiana Stable H.S. Clark (Christiana Stables) **113**

1968	4	1	0	0	$2,760
1967	0	M	0	0	–

3Jun68–3Del	fst 6f	$.22\frac{2}{5}$	$.46\frac{3}{5}$	1.12	Md Sp Wt	11	11	$9^{7\frac{1}{2}}$	$3^{5\frac{1}{2}}$	2^{1}	$1^{\frac{1}{2}}$	B Thornburg	b 113	7.10	85-20	Full Reach $113^{\frac{1}{2}}$ Noble's Mill 113^{7} Fleet Change 110^{5}	Driving	12
29Apr68–4Pim	fst 6f	.23	$.46\frac{4}{5}$	1.14	Md Sp Wt	8	6	$7^{8\frac{1}{4}}$	9^{12}	9^{11}	$10^{8\frac{1}{2}}$	O Rosado	112	5.50	71-17	Withering Fire 111no Sam Bolero $114^{\frac{3}{4}}$ King's Shilling 112^{h}	Far back	12
13Apr68–6GP	fst 7f	$.22\frac{3}{5}$	$.45\frac{2}{5}$	$1.22\frac{4}{5}$	Allowance	12	2	$7^{3\frac{3}{4}}$	$6^{4\frac{1}{2}}$	$4^{7\frac{1}{2}}$	7^{13}	O Rosado	114	14.40	82-18	Mineola Lad 114^{8} Globesona 117no Patricia G. G. $107^{1\frac{1}{2}}$	No mishap	12
29Mar68–4GP	fst 7f	$.22\frac{3}{5}$	$.45\frac{4}{5}$	1.25	Md Sp Wt	9	3	$3^{1\frac{1}{2}}$	$4^{7\frac{1}{2}}$	$5^{6\frac{1}{2}}$	$4^{5\frac{3}{4}}$	O Rosado	120	10.40	78-16	Directive $120^{1\frac{3}{4}}$ Precious Boy 120^{1} Video Gold 120^{3}	In close	12

LATEST WORKOUTS **Jun 1 Del 5f sl 1.04 b** **May 27 Del 5f fst 1.02 b** **May 23 Del 4f fst $.48\frac{3}{5}$ h** **May 11 Pim 6f fst $1.16\frac{2}{5}$ b**

surface for that race was fast; "6f" was the distance—6 furlongs, or ¾ mile. (A furlong is ⅛ mile.)

Then come the fractional times of the leading horse or horses in Full Reach's last race. The figures *.22 2/5, .46 3/5* and *1.12* mean that the lead horse ran the first quarter-mile of the race in 22 2/5 seconds, the half-mile in 46 3/5 seconds and the ¾ mile in 1 minute and 12 seconds. Since the race was 6 furlongs, one minute and 12 seconds was also the final running time.

"Md Sp Wt" was the class of race in Full Reach's last start. It means "maiden special weight," an event for horses that have never won. If it had been a claiming race the abbreviation would have been "Clm" and Full Reach's claiming price would have been given.

Then comes Full Reach's progress in the race. The first number, *11,* means that he started from post position 11. The next *11* was his position behind the leader as the horses left the post. The numbers *7½* mean that the quarter-mile point of the race Full Reach was ninth, 7½ (raised numbers) lengths behind the lead horse. Following the line across, you'll see that at the half-mile mark he was third, 5½ lengths behind the leader and at the start of the homestretch he'd moved up to second, only 1 length out of first. The final number in that series, *1½,* means that Full Reach won the race by one-half length.

"BThornburg" was Full Reach's jockey. The letter "b" that follows means he wore blinkers in that race. Next comes his weight assignment, 113 pounds. "7.10" is his equivalent odds in the race—$7.10 to $1. "85–20" were the speed rating and track variant of his performance, both of which I will explain later. After that are the names of the top three horses in that race, their weights and the distance they finished in front of the horse behind them.

"Driving" is the paper's description of Full Reach's performance in the race. As is easily seen by the outcome, it means he finished the race with a late charge.

The final "12" on the line means it was a twelve-horse field.

At the bottom of Full Reach's performance listings are his latest workouts. The notation "Jun 1 Del 5f sl 1.04 b" means that his last recorded workout was on June 1 at Delaware Park, that he went five furlongs over a slow (sl) track in the time of 1 minute, 4 seconds, and that he was "breezing" (b), or running full-out.

I prefer the *Telegraph* over the *Form* because its past-performance listings give running times beginning with the ¼-mile mark of most races, while the *Form* only gives times from the ½-mile mark. I find the ¼-mile running time very useful in my calculations.

The *Telegraph* and the *Form* don't list scratches or official jockeys for the day's races. You get this information from the official program at the track or you can buy one of the "scratch sheets" that give that data at your newsstand. I suggest you try to obtain this information as early as possible so you can include it in your prerace study.

Allow yourself at least two hours of study before you get to the track. Most tracks run nine races a day, with eight to fourteen horses in each race. That means you'll be faced with about 100 horses in your day at the track, and two hours is the minimum you'll need to give each horse its proper attention.

Prerace study is vital because you'll have other things to do in the 25 to 30 minutes between races. In that period you should be watching the horses as they come out for the next race and reviewing your calculations on the race that has just been run. If you've won the previous race or your horse ran a close second or third, you won't have to do much rechecking. If you were far off, it's a good idea to try to figure out where you went wrong. Did your horse encounter interference so that he couldn't find running room? That's bad riding, or bad racing luck, and it's not your fault. Or did you misjudge the condition of the track—is it really "fast" as posted, or did the time of the race indicate that the going is a bit heavy under the surface? If the track seems a bit heavy, take another look at your figures.

Then there is the matter of attitude. A good handicapper must be both firm and flexible. This sounds contradictory, but it isn't. By firmness I mean that you should come to the track with your top selections clearly marked in every race, and you shouldn't be easily swayed from them, especially by the odds-board. Don't be caught in the rush to bet on the favorite if he didn't look like a winner in your prerace analysis. The favorite saying of my good friend Julie Fink, one of the best handicappers around, is, "The public makes the favorites and the public usually is wrong." Julie knows what he is talking about. Statistics show that favorites win only about one-third of the time, but at odds unfavorable to coming out ahead. If you like a horse that opens at 3–1 and goes to 5–1 or 6–1 while the public pushes another horse down to even money, smile. Think of the return you will get if you are right. Have confidence in your own ability.

By flexibility I mean you must have the capacity to alter your plans if you see something on which you hadn't counted. Notice I said "see," not "hear." For example, a horse you thought deserved a bet comes out on the track wearing front-leg bandages that he didn't wear his last time out. Watch this horse closely. If he doesn't warm up properly, keep your money in your pocket.

Changes in the odds may affect your plans within certain limits. For instance, you may see the odds drop very low on a horse you'd planned to bet—so low that you begin to wonder if the return will justify the risk of your money. When the odds on your horse dip below 2–1, be sure your horse looks at least two lengths better than the field before you bet. When the odds go below even-money, I generally advise no bet at all. Rare is the horse that will persuade me to risk more money than I will get back if he wins.

On the other hand, you may notice that the odds have risen sharply on a horse you like as a second or third choice. Again, watch this horse closely while he warms up. If you don't see anything disturbing, you might want to bet a few dollars on him in addition to your planned bet.

In brief, don't come to the track with your mind so set it can't be changed by what you see.

To summarize:

1. Don't look for sure-fire "systems" for picking winners—they don't exist.

2. Allow at least two hours for your prerace study of the *Morning Telegraph* or the *Daily Racing Form.*

3. Be confident of your selections, but be flexible. Believe what you see, not what you hear.

4. If you want to bet on a horse going off at odds of between 2–1 and even-money, make sure he looks like a solid winner. As a rule, don't take less than even-money.

Pace Makes the Race

Now to get down to specifics. There is one maxim I invariably follow in my handicapping, indeed, it's the keystone of my method. It is: *Pace makes the race.* By "pace makes the race"

I mean that *the manner in which a race is run determines its outcome.* In most races, two types of horses stand a chance to win—"speed" horses and those that prefer to come from behind late in the race. A speed horse isn't necessarily one that must lead all the way. It is a horse that likes to run "on the pace"; that is, within five lengths of the leaders in the early stages of the race.

Speed that goes unchallenged almost invariably wins. If a horse's past performances show that his times in the early portions of his races are clearly better than those of his competitors, the chances are great that he will open up a commanding lead and his late-running rivals will not be able to catch him. When you see a situation like this, you needn't go further. Unless he clearly lacks stamina, the speed horse is the horse for you to bet.

Mostly, however, speed does not go unchallenged. In most races, there are two or even three horses with enough early speed to challenge one another. This often means that the race will be run at a very fast pace, and the speed horses will tire themselves in their early battling. If none of the speed horses in the field has clearly shown that he has the capacity to stand off early challenges and still win, you should bring the come-from-behind horses into your calculations.

Looking at the past-performance charts with these factors in mind, you will be able to form a mental picture of the manner in which the race will be run. Using the horses' fractional times from their past races, which your study of the *Telegraph* or *Racing Form* will give you, try to visualize which horse or horses will take the early lead and which horses, if any, will make late bids. Use paper and pencil to write all this down. Bet on the horse that emerges the winner in this prerace analysis.

I think a partly hypothetical example will help explain what

I mean about pace in a race. The chart on page 73 describes the running of the June 8, 1968, Oceanport Handicap at Monmouth Park. Because of the large field of entries, the race was divided into two divisions of seven horses each, with $18,046 going to each winner.

Incidentally, there is one important difference in reading charts of race results and past-performance listings. In the past performances, a horse's position is given in terms of his distance behind the *lead* horse; the numbers 6 10, for instance, would mean the horse was sixth, 10 lengths *behind* the leader. In race-results charts, such as that below, however, horses are ranked in their position *ahead* of the next horse. In the chart below, Burning Bridges, at the quarter-mile mark (¼ on the top-line guide) is listed as 3^2, which means he was third, 2 lengths *ahead of the fourth horse*. To see how far from the lead he was, add the lengths between the horses in front of him. You'll see that Country Friend was first at that point by 4 lengths and Streakie II, who finished last, was second by 3. That means Burning Bridges was 7 lengths off the lead at the quarter.

Both divisions of the Oceanport were run at one mile over the turf course. In the first division of the stake, Country Friend, a fine six-year-old horse and an 11–10 favorite in the betting, was an easy winner. He was a horse of great speed. He was in the No. 1 post position, and the run into the first turn at a mile is short on Monmouth's grass course. Thus he had no trouble clearing his field early. He was 4 lengths ahead at the quarter, 4 at the half, 2 at the three-quarter and won by 4. The second-place horse, Burning Bridges, made up some ground late in the race, but not enough. It was a clear case of speed going unchallenged. The final running time was 1:36 3/5, only 1/5 second off the course record.

SEVENTH RACE

Mth – 34961

JUNE 8, 1968

1 MILE (Turf). (Lucky Turn, June 10, 1967, 1.36$\frac{2}{5}$, 7, 118.) Twenty-second running. THE OCEANPORT HANDICAP. $25,000 added. (First division). 3-years-olds and upward. By subscription of $25 each, $100 to pass the entry box, and $150 additional to start. The added money and all fees to be divided 65% to the winner, 20% to second, 10% to third, and 5% to fourth. Closed with 73 nominations.

Value of race $27,762.50. Value to winner $18,045.63, second $5,552.50, third $2,776.25, fourth $1,388.12. Mutuel pool $259,222.

Index	Horse	Eqt	A	Wt	PP	St	¼	½	¾	Str	Fin	Jockey	Owner	Odds $1
34805GS^1	Country Friend	b	6	116	1	1	1^4	1^4	1^2	1^4	1^4	J Vasquez	Circle M Farm	1.10
34631GS^2	Burning Bridges		4	111	3	2	3^2	3^1	3^1	2^4	$2^{1\frac{3}{4}}$	D Hidalgo	Tartan Stable	2.80
34752GS^3	Vis-A-Vis	b	5	109	5	5	5^2	5^1	$4^{1\frac{1}{2}}$	3^2	3^4	V Tejada	Flo-Henny Stable	20.50
34725Aqu^1	Boyinahurry		3	109	4	3	$4^{1\frac{1}{2}}$	$4^{1\frac{1}{2}}$	5^2	$4^{1\frac{1}{2}}$	4^2	C Barrera	Mrs W Gilroy	4.70
34499GP^4	Proud Sailor		4	111	6	6	6^h	7	$6^{\frac{1}{2}}$	$6^{\frac{1}{2}}$	$5^{\frac{3}{4}}$	C Baltazar	Mrs R L Reineman	17.90
34606Bel^7	Voluntario III		7	112	7	7	7	6^h	7	7	6^3	W Gavidia	Crown Stable	6.60
Eng 67	Streakie II		4	109	2	4	2^3	2^7	2^2	$5^{\frac{1}{2}}$	7	W Tichenor	Mrs W C Wright	29.40

Time .24, .47$\frac{1}{5}$, 1.11$\frac{3}{5}$, 1.36$\frac{3}{5}$. Track firm.

$2 Mutuel Prices:

2–COUNTRY FRIEND	4.20	3.00	2.80
4–BURNING BRIDGES		3.20	3.00
6–VIS-A-VIS			4.40

B. g, by Olympia–Molly Barker, by Errard. Trainer J. Long. Bred by J. W. Galbreath.

IN GATE AT 5.00. OFF AT 5.00 EASTERN DAYLIGHT TIME. Start good. Won driving.

COUNTRY FRIEND had his speed to take the early lead, saved ground on the clubhouse turn, jumped a shadow nearing the four and a half-furlong grounds, recovered quickly to maintain a long lead and was not menaced while kept to pressure to the end. BURNING BRIDGES could not stay with pace early, rallied leaving the backstretch and finished evenly. VIS-A-VIS was no match for the top pair while clearly best of the others. BOYINAHURRY was never a factor. VOLUNTARIO III was always outrun. STREAKIE II made a mild bid into the stretch and flattened out.

Scratched – 34769GS^4 Make It. Overweights – Proud Sailor 1 pound, Voluntario III 3.

3-year-olds and upward. By subscription of $25 each, $100 to pass the entry box, and $150 additional to start. The added money and all fees to be divided 65% to the winner, 20% to second, 10% to third, and 5% to fourth. Closed with 73 nominations.

Value of race $27,762.50. Value to winner $18,045.63, second $5,552.50, third $2,776.25, fourth $1,388.12. Mutuel pool $285,395.

Index	Horse	Eqt	A	Wt	PP	St	¼	½	¾	Str	Fin	Jockey	Owner	Odds $1
34653AP^4	Quite An Accent	b	5	113	3	2	2^1	2^h	$3^{1\frac{1}{2}}$	1^1	1^3	BTh'burg	Bwamazon Farm	6.40
34907Bel^1	More Scents		4	117	5	4	3^2	$3^{1\frac{1}{2}}$	$2^{\frac{1}{2}}$	$3^{1\frac{1}{2}}$	$2^{1\frac{3}{4}}$	JVelasquez	Meadowhill	1.40
34908Del^3	Tornum	b	5	112	6	7	6^2	$4^{\frac{1}{2}}$	$4^{1\frac{1}{2}}$	4^5	$3^{1\frac{1}{2}}$	PKallai	Mrs W C Wright	9.20
34908Del^{11}	Road At Sea	b	4	120	1	1	$1^{1\frac{1}{2}}$	1^2	$1^{1\frac{1}{2}}$	$2^{\frac{1}{2}}$	4^1	CBurr	Mrs Henry Obre	2.00
34805GS^7	Shooting Chant		4	108	7	6	5^h	6^4	5^3	$5^{\frac{1}{2}}$	5^4	MMiceli	San Marco Stable	25.90
34752GS^2	Gallant Moment	b	4	116	2	3	$4^{1\frac{1}{2}}$	5^h	$6^{1\frac{1}{2}}$	$6^{\frac{1}{2}}$	6^1	DKassen	Circle M Farm	13.20
34908Del^5	Pistacho II		6	112	4	5	7	7	7	7	7	WGavidia	Mrs F I Guerini	9.90

Time .24, .47$\frac{2}{5}$, 1.11$\frac{2}{5}$, 1.36$\frac{2}{5}$ (equals course record). Track firm.

$2 Mutuel Prices:

4–QUITE AN ACCENT	14.80	5.00	3.60
6–MORE SCENTS		3.00	2.60
7–TORNUM			3.40

Ch. g, by King of the Tudors–Bamboo Hut, by Polynesian. Bred by C. P. Sanborn. Trainer Bwamazon Farm (Ky.).

IN GATE AT 5.31. OFF AT 5.31 EASTERN DAYLIGHT TIME. Start good. Won driving.

QUITE AN ACCENT, well placed and in hand to the end of the backstretch, rallied between horses to take command settling for the drive and drew out under hustling tactics. MORE SCENTS, never far back, moved up outside QUITE AN ACCENT on the turn then could not stay with that one in the drive. TORNUM was sent up behind the leaders leaving the quarter mile grounds and faltered. ROAD AT SEA sprinted clear from the inside in the run to the clubhouse turn, held away to the stretch and tired. PISTACHO II was always outrun.

Scratched – 34679Bel^1 High Hat. Overweight – Pistacho II, 1 pound.

The second part of the Oceanport was run differently. There were three horses in the race with considerable early speed: Road At Sea, out of post position No. 1; More Scents, from No. 5; and Quite An Accent, from No. 3. Road At Sea broke first and clipped off the first three-quarter mile in a time slightly faster than Country Friend's, but More Scents and Quite An Accent were right with him. Quite An Accent gained the lead in the stretch and drew away to win. His time equaled the course record. Road At Sea finished fourth.

Now, what would have happened if all fourteen of those horses had gone to the post together? On the basis of final times alone, Quite An Accent would have been the winner, and Country Friend would have been a close second. But I don't think it would have worked that way. Country Friend, Road At Sea, More Scents and Quite An Accent are all speed horses. If they had run together, the early pace would have been terrific—even faster than it was in either actual race. I would have bet on Burning Bridges, who in several past races had shown the ability to win from off the pace. I think he would have been the only horse with anything left in the stretch. The running time of my hypothetical combined race might well have been *slower* than that of either actual race. A sizzling-fast early pace has a tiring effect on horses, and this often produces a slow final quarter-mile in a 1-mile race. I think the field would have "come back" to Burning Bridges in that final quarter-mile. The pace of the race would have made him the winner.

Sometimes a race will defy your ability to evaluate it. Even after forty years at the races, this still happens to me. Under those conditions, I don't bet. It's no crime to "pass" an occasional race; in fact, it's a necessity for financial success. I rarely play every race on a day's card.

To summarize:

1. Speed unchallenged almost invariably wins.

2. When several horses appear likely to stage a tiring battle for the early lead, look for a come-from-behind horse.

3. Don't be ashamed not to bet on a race if it defies your ability to analyze it.

Time

The handicapper usually has to make some adjustments when he tries to evaluate horses' times in their past races. This is because the newspaper race charts and past-performance listings on individual animals give only the fractional times of the leading horse and the winner's final running time. Unless your horse led all the way, you will have to employ the formula that relates lengths on the track to seconds on the clock. The formula is simple: 5 lengths equals one second, or 1 length equals 1/5 second.

The accompanying chart is for Parida, a three-year-old filly, as she went into the 1⅛ mile $75,000 Mother Goose Stakes at Belmont Park on June 8, 1968. In her previous race, shown in the top line below her name, Parida finished fourth by 5 lengths (4⁵) to a winner who covered 6 furlongs, or ¾ mile, in 1:10 3/5. Using the 5-lengths-to-a-second formula, this means Parida's final time in the race was 1:11 3/5. Before the final time of 1:10 3/5 in the chart is the time :44 1/5. That is the half-mile time in the race. At that point, Parida was eighth, 6¾ lengths behind the leading horse. That means her running time for the half-mile was roughly :45 3/5, adding 7 lengths, or 1 2/5 seconds, to the leader's time.

Another formula in adjusting running times takes into con-

Parida* Ch. f (1965–Ky), by Parade–Queen's Mount, by Royal Charger

I. Bieber J. W. Jacobs (Erdenheim Farms Co.)

121

1968	8	3	2	1	$25,219
1967	0	M	0	0	–

1Jun68–8Mth	fst 6f	.21$\frac{1}{5}$	.44$\frac{1}{5}$	1.10$\frac{3}{5}$	f– MWoodfd	10	7	$10^{9\frac{3}{4}}$	10^{11}	$8^{6\frac{3}{4}}$	4^{5}	CBaltazar	116	15.10	84–15	First Noel 116^{2} Twice Cited $116^{\frac{1}{2}}$ Singing Tune $114^{2\frac{1}{2}}$	Late foot 10
27May68–8Bel	fst 6f	.22$\frac{2}{5}$	.45$\frac{3}{5}$	1.11$\frac{1}{5}$	f– Allow	3	5	$5^{4\frac{1}{2}}$	5^{6}	6^{4}	2^{1}	JLRotz	114	3.10	90–14	WildBeauty 114^{1} Parida 114^{nk} Teddy's True 110^{2}	Finished fast 8
8May68–7Aqu	fst 7f	.21$\frac{3}{5}$	.44$\frac{2}{5}$	1.22$\frac{2}{5}$	f– Comely	7	5	9^{10}	9^{10}	$9^{5\frac{1}{4}}$	$8^{7\frac{3}{4}}$	RTurcotte	112	6.90e	86–11	Best In Show 112no Heartland 113^{2} Gay Matelda 115^{2}	No factor 11
17Apr68–7Aqu	fst 7f	.22$\frac{4}{5}$	.45$\frac{3}{5}$	1.23$\frac{4}{5}$	f– Allow	2	5	3^{nk}	2^{h}	2^{h}	2^{nk}	AGarramone[5]	107	*2.00	87–17	Best In Show 112^{nk} Parida $107^{1\frac{1}{2}}$ Teddy's True 112^{2}	Held gamely 8
2Apr68–7Aqu	fst 6f	.22$\frac{3}{5}$	.46	1.11	f– Allow	4	5	3^{1}	2^{1}	3^{3}	$3^{3\frac{1}{2}}$	JCruguet	112	*0.40	84–21	Intensely 118^{2} Clems Fairy Gold $118^{1\frac{1}{2}}$ Parida 112^{6}	Tired 5
26Mar68–6Aqu	fst 7f	.23	.45$\frac{2}{5}$	1.23$\frac{4}{5}$	f– Allow	4	2	1^{h}	1^{1}	1^{2}	1^{3}	JCruguet	110	*0.30	87–18	Parida 110^{3} Clems Fairy Gold 120^{4} Brookbridge 112^{2}	Easily 5
20Mar68–6Aqu	gd 7f	.23$\frac{3}{5}$	.47$\frac{1}{5}$	1.24$\frac{3}{5}$	f– Allow	2	4	2^{h}	$1^{\frac{1}{2}}$	1^{3}	1^{6}	JCruguet	112	2.60	83–24	Parida 112^{6} Sweeping Wing $113^{3\frac{1}{2}}$ Tiger Balm 112^{3}	Easily best 6
13Mar68–4Aqu	sly 6f	.23	.47$\frac{2}{5}$	1.13$\frac{4}{5}$	f– MdSpWt	7	5	Snow		$1^{\frac{1}{2}}$	$1^{2\frac{1}{2}}$	JCruguet	121	21.30	74–25	Parida $121^{2\frac{1}{2}}$ Sequela $114^{\frac{1}{2}}$ Mertensia $121^{2\frac{1}{2}}$	Driving clear 12

LATEST WORKOUTS **Jun 7 Aqu 3f fst .38 b** **May 25 Aqu 4f sly .47$\frac{1}{5}$ h** **May 22 Aqu 4f fst .49 b** **May 18 Aqu 4f fst .49 b**

sideration the weight a horse carries. Five pounds of additional weight on a horse is supposed to add 1 length, or 1/5 second, to his time over the mile; conversely, five pounds less should reduce that time by 1/5 second. On Parida's chart, you'll notice that she carried 116 pounds in her last race over the three-quarter mile. In the Mother Goose, she was to carry 121 pounds over 1⅛ miles. Because weight takes its toll mostly at longer-distance races, the extra five pounds should add a length or two to her form over the longer distance.

Speed Chart Handicappers

There are men around the tracks known as "speed-chart" handicappers who base their calculations on a combination of running times, weights and track condition. The latter factor is especially important in their system. Most horses run best on "fast" tracks—those which are dry and firm. If a track is the least bit soft, it will show up in slower running times for the day. The *Morning Telegraph* and *Racing Form* compute a track "variant" each day for each track, and include it in the past-performance listings of the horses. In that calculation, track-record times are ranked as 100, or "par." The average winning times for all races on a given day are taken, and the difference between this and 100 is the track variant. One "point" in the variant formula equals 1/5 second. Thus if the average winning time for a day's races is two seconds slower than the track records for the various distances, the track variant would be 10.

Some speed-chart men use the newspapers' track-variant rating and others compute their own. If the track is fast the day they are doing their betting and a horse has run in a certain time recently over a slightly slower track, they will subtract fractions of a second off that time. If the track is slower that day than it was in the horse's previous outing, they will add fractions. They then introduce weights into their figures, and arrive at a final speed rating for each horse. The horse with the best rating gets their bets.

The speed-chart men have gone about as far as possible toward putting handicapping on a scientific basis. Some of them have been successful. However, I do not agree completely with their method. As far as I am concerned, final running time can be the biggest liar in the game. It is useful as a guide, but no more than that. If horses ran true to time, the game would be a simple one. It isn't. Even the best horses are basically inconsistent animals. The final times they post are greatly affected by the manner in which their races are run. A horse can win in very impressive time because his speed goes unchallenged, then come right back and lose in much slower time because he is bothered by his competition. In another case, two horses in a race might have won their previous starts, one easily and the other with difficulty but in slightly faster time. When they meet, I'll take the easy winner in the slower time. I believe an easy win perks up a horse; a difficult win takes something out of him, no matter how fast his final time.

Another kind of running time bettors must deal with comes in workouts. Generally, you can chop two seconds off a horse's workout clocking and get a fair approximation of how he would have performed in an actual race. However, workouts can be deceiving and should be taken with a grain of salt. A good example of this occurred in June, 1968, at Arlington Park in Chicago. Verbatim went a mile in preparation for the $100,000 Arlington Classic in a sensational 1:34 3/5, only two seconds over Buckpasser's then-world-record time for the distance. In the actual race four days later, Verbatim finished a poor seventh to a winner who was clocked in an unspectacular 1:36.

Workout times can be misleading for reasons other than the basic inconsistencies of horses. Many tracks are not rigorous in their standards for registering and clocking horses that appear for workouts. Thus some workouts go unrecorded and others are timed in a slap-dash manner. Santa Anita Park, near Los Angeles, requires trainers who work out their horses to so inform track officials, and Santa Anita employs its own workout-clockers instead of leaving that up to the newspapers. I would like to see more tracks follow Santa Anita's example.

To summarize:

1. In computing horses' running times, 5 lengths on the track equals one second on the clock.

2. Five pounds of additional weight on a horse should add 1 length, or 1/5 second, to his running time over 1 mile. Conversely, five pounds less should reduce his time by 1/5 second at that distance.

3. Final running time can be a liar; it is affected considerably by the manner in which the race was run. A horse that has just won an easy race should get an edge over the recent winner of a difficult race, even though his final running time was slightly slower.

4. Take workout times with a grain of salt.

Class

Most of all, the way a race is run is determined by the "class" of the competition. To a certain extent, class is determined for the bettor by the way tracks organize races to make competition fairly equal.

The most common race is the claiming race, in which the price of the animals acts as the equalizer. In order to enter his horse in a claiming race, an owner must put a price tag on him and prior to the race offer him for sale to any other owner with a horse registered in the same meeting. If a claim (purchase order) is placed on a horse, the animal goes to the claimant after the race, regardless of how he finishes or his physical condition. The purse, if any, goes to the original owner. Usually, no more than $1,000 separates the claiming prices of horses in the same race. The possibility of losing horses keeps owners from entering valuable animals in cheap claiming races they could certainly win.

A step above the claimer is the allowance race, in which competition is equalized by giving lower weight assignments to horses that haven't won a designated number of races or amount of money within stated periods of time. Recent winners thus carry top weights, while horses with poor recent records carry less and have an improved chance of winning.

The third broad class of race is the stakes race. Stakes (the term derives from "sweepstakes") races attract the best horses, partly because owners must put up their own money in entry fees in order to gain places for their horses. Horses must usually be nominated for stakes races well in advance of the actual running date. Additional entry fees are charged to owners of nominees as race day approaches. Some owners will pay the fees for the honor of having one of their horses in a prestigious event. However, the fees and the generally high level of competition usually restrict stakes fields to top-grade animals.

There are, of course, differences in class within these race groupings, and this is where differences of definition enter. In this sense, "class" is the most abused word on the tracks. To some sportswriters a class horse is one that belongs to a blueblood owner, or one that was purchased for a very high price in a yearling sale by virtue of having illustrious forebears. Breeding is an important element in determining a horse's class, but to evaluate an animal on the basis of the social position of his owner or his original purchase price is ridiculous. In the first place, horses are colorblind, so they can't see whose silks they are carrying. They don't know if they are running for Alfred Gwynne Vanderbilt or Sam Lewin. Secondly, many, many horses who sell for $50,000 and up in yearling sales never win more than cheap claiming races.

Often a horse stepping down in company—either in claiming price or type of race—will quickly get the tag "class of the race." Such a horse indeed may be the class of his field, but only if his record warrants it. Many times you will see a horse drop into the claiming class from the allowance or stakes ranks. When you examine his record, you'll see that the only reason he was run so high in the first place was to justify his owner's poor purchase decision. After many losing efforts in good company, the owner will decide that his horse is really a "dog," and he'll put him in a claiming race in the hope that someone will buy him. You can recognize this horse by seeing that he's been beaten by furlongs, not just lengths, in his previous starts. This horse may get the "class" tag, but he won't deserve it.

On the other hand, watch closely for horses that step down after performing *creditably* in better company. Horses don't have to win to perform well. A horse can be beaten by 2 lengths, 3 lengths or even 5 lengths and still have run a good race. He tried to win, but his competition was too good. When a horse like this is dropped to a lower level, he deserves a close look. He may even deserve the "class" tag. But such instances are rarer than you think. As a rule, I favor a horse that is improving and stepping up in company after several victories over one who is stepping down after a string of defeats. Winning and losing both get to be habits with horses. I prefer horses with good habits.

Class in horses, then, is partly the ability to win. A horse who can be counted on for a good effort wherever he is placed (within reason) exhibits class. Class also is consistency. This, as much as sheer speed, is what separates the ordinary horses from the good ones. Claiming horses, even cheap ones, sometimes possess speed and a fair will to win. Their lack of consistency puts them in the claiming class.

Importance of Consistency

Consistency is what makes betting on allowance and stakes races easier than betting on claiming races. The higher up in class you go, the more formful the races become. By "formful" I mean that the horses are likely to finish in the order that their past performances indicate. When you see a race full of $3,500 claiming horses, it's always difficult to pick a winner because you don't know how they'll perform on a given day. Stakes and allowance-class horses run much closer to form, so your chances are better of being right with your bet.

You might ask how horses know when they are running out of their class. The other horses let them know. That's an important reason why time is such a liar. Horses placed with competition that's too good for them rarely perform as well as they do at lower levels. I learned this lesson the hard way early in my career. I had claimed the colt Deserter for $1,250 for the Paragon Stable in 1937. He had plenty of speed. One reason he was available so cheaply was that he was a notoriously bad post horse—he didn't always leave the gate well. But if he started right, he could run quite well.

I was so impressed with Deserter's speed that immediately after I bought him I stepped him off in a claiming race for $5,000 horses; allowing for inflation, a $5,000 horse of the early 1930s is the equivalent of a $15,000 horse today. Deserter's running times compared favorably with his opposition in that race. I went so far as to bet on him.

My rider that day was a promising young jockey named Eddie Arcaro. He was intelligent even early in his career. "Aren't you running this horse a little high?" he asked before the race.

"This horse has good speed," I said. "There's no reason he can't take this race. Get him into the lead and see how he does."

Arcaro made a good effort with Deserter. He got him out of the gate in good style. But he never could get him in front. None of the early speed Deserter had shown in his previous, cheaper races materialized. The other horses wore him to a frazzle, and he finished far in the rear in his worst time ever. Later, when I ran him at $2,000 and $2,500, he reverted to form and did better. But in the high-priced race, those other horses must have said a few things to poor Deserter.

To summarize:

1. Horses that are consistent and show the ability to win exhibit class.

2. The higher the class of race, the better your chance of being right with your bet.

3. Watch for horses that drop down in class after performing creditably at a higher level. Nevertheless, favor horses that are improving and stepping up moderately in class over those that are stepping down after a string of defeats.

4. Horses put with competition that's much too good for them rarely perform as well as they have at cheaper levels.

Weight

Evaluating the importance of weight in a race is much easier than evaluating class. You already know the rule of thumb relating pounds to running time: Five pounds over 1 mile equals 1 length, or 1/5 seconds. In practice, I pay little attention to weight in races of less than a mile, and even then it enters my calculations mainly when I am trying to decide between two horses that seem to be fairly equal in ability.

The importance of weight in longer races is easy to explain. A five-pound weight in your pocket won't bother you at all if you are running only one block, but it may slow you down a step or two at two blocks. The longer you run, the more burdensome the weight becomes. In long horse races—1⅛ miles or more—I figure that five pounds equals 1½ or 2 lengths, and virtually all of that comes in the final quarter-mile or so.

Weight shouldn't be a strong consideration when you are trying to match horses of widely unequal ability. There is a saying around the tracks that "weight can stop a train." I don't buy it. If my horse is 10 lengths better than yours, you can put 140 pounds on mine and 100 pounds on yours and I will still beat you over any standard distance. I won't beat you by 10 lengths, but I'll beat you by 4 or 5. It would be another instance of class winning out.

Sometimes you will come across a race in which there is very little difference between two horses. Let's assume that the two horses have met before in a mile race. Horse A, carrying 115 pounds, beat horse B, carrying 112 pounds, by a head. This time, over the same distance, horse A is carrying 116 pounds and horse B 111 pounds. On the basis of weight, that should put B's nose in front of A at the wire. Possibly, but not necessarily. I would say that A gained a psychological edge by beating B that last time out, and it would probably compensate for the additional difference of two pounds.

However, if A were made to carry 118 pounds in that return race and B were dropped to 110 pounds, I'd have to give the nod to B. In my opinion, that's enough of a weight advantage to make a difference in such a case, all other things being equal. It takes a fairly considerable change of weight to make one horse beat another that has beaten him recently.

To summarize:

1. The importance of weight increases with the distance of the race.

2. Weight differences shouldn't figure importantly in your calculations of races of less than 1 mile.

3. Weight is important mainly in deciding between horses of fairly equal ability.

4. A change of one or two pounds usually won't reverse a finish in a rematch of a recent, close race.

Post Position

Of far more importance than weight in my method of handicapping is post position. Many times, the difference between a horse finishing first or seventh in a race is the position from which he starts. In the chapter on tracks we will deal with special post-position situations at specific tracks. Here we shall deal with general guidelines. Observation of the conditions at the tracks you attend will enable you to judge if my guides hold true for you.

Three things make post position an important factor in a race: the length of the race, the contour of the track and the distance into the first turn. At distances of 1⅛ miles or greater, post position usually has little bearing on the outcome of a race because the distance is long enough for each horse to settle into the running position that suits him best.

Post position comes into play most strongly in races where the run into the first turn is short—¼ mile or less. In this sort of race inside post positions are advantageous to both speed horses and horses that like to come from behind. This goes double for tracks such as Tropical Park in Miami, where the turns are sharply angled.

The most important question a handicapper must ask himself when evaluating a speed horse's chances is whether the horse can clear his field early and move smartly into the pace. In races where the run into the first turn is short, this is very difficult to do from the outside. A speed horse stationed on the outside of his field must run faster and farther to reach the pace than a speed horse starting from the inside. This early run will drain the horse physically, leaving him tired later in the race.

The same holds true for come-from-behind horses in races run into a close first turn. The late-running horse must attempt to save ground along the rail early in a race in order to have enough strength left for his late burst. Starting from the outside, this horse will find many other horses between himself and the rail. A jockey will almost have to pull up this horse when he leaves the gate and swing him around in back of the field in order to reach the rail. This is likely to put the horse off stride. The jockey's alternative is to shoot his horse past the pack to the rail and then slow him down. This is equally undesirable because it requires a strong early run, which is contrary to the horse's style. It takes a strong late runner to overcome an outside post position, especially in races of ¾ mile or less.

Many tracks have chutes extending off their main track, from which they start races of ¾ mile to 1 mile. These chutes provide a long run into the first turn. This makes the situation for speed horses different from what it is in races where the first-turn run is short. Coming out of a chute, speed horses do better from the outside post positions. Here, getting stuck outside on the first turn is no problem. The speed horse on the outside has ample room in which to clear his field and settle into the pace before the distant first turn is reached. The going is often toughest along the rail, where several horses will be vying for position.

Late-running horses tend to do better from the inside coming out of the chute for the ground-saving reasons already stated.

Post position is also important in another situation. If two speed horses are stationed next to each other in the starting gate, the chances are considerable that they will battle themselves into exhaustion early and be overtaken by a late runner. This holds true even if the two speed horses are separated by one horse in the gate: for examples, if they start from positions 1 and 3, or 2 and 4.

To summarize:

1. Post position usually means little in races of 1⅛ miles or more.

2. In races where the run into the first turn is short—¼ mile or less—inside post positions are best. This is especially true in races of ¾ mile or less, and at tracks where the turns are sharply angled.

3. Outside post positions usually help "speed" horses in races from chutes.

4. Beware of betting on a speed horse placed in the starting gate alongside another speed horse of similar ability.

In and Out of Form

The vast majority of horses do not run well month in and month out. The few who do are great champions, and you will have no trouble spotting them. The rest—perhaps 95 percent—run well for a while and then ease off for a while. This is known as being "in" or "out" of form.

Don't attempt to judge a horse's ability on one race alone, but one race *can* indicate a turn in a horse's form. Usually, unless an injury intervenes, horses' upturns continue for five or six races. In years past, ordinary horses could maintain their improvement over more races than they can today. This is because track surfaces are harder than they used to be and horses are raced more frequently. Horses that should be resting or recuperating are made to race, and this affects their form—for the worse.

Many handicappers are inclined to "throw out"—completely discount—a race that is sharply better or worse than the horse usually runs. I am not one of those. I am very anxious to see the way that horse runs the next time out. If the unusual effort was better than past performances and it is repeated soon afterward, the horse deserves much attention—he's definitely on the upturn. If the unusual effort is poorer than past performances, one more race should tell whether the horse is physically sound. If you see a normally good horse come up with two bad efforts in a row, don't look for any quick improvement. Normally that's a sign he needs rest on a farm.

The unusual races I *do* throw out are those run in the mud—over tracks which are classed as slow, muddy or heavy. Races are not truly run in the mud. Whether the horse wins or loses in the mud makes no difference to me. If he comes back on a fast track, I will discount his mud race. I will look to see the way he ran when the track was "fast."

A horse's recent form—his last three or four races—is far more important to me than how he ran three or four months before. I am no waker of the dead. Many times, in order to justify a selection, a bettor will point to a good effort a horse made ten races back and assert that this is the horse's "true" form. Not so. In this day of hard tracks and hard racing, a good horse can become physically unsound overnight. Recent form will provide the best clue to his present condition.

To summarize:

1. Don't judge a horse's ability on one race alone, but be alert for upturns or downturns in his form.

2. When handicapping for a fast track, throw out horses' mud races.

3. Base your bet on a horse's last three or four races.

Track Conditions

A change in track conditions can be fatal to the best-laid plans of the handicapper. On the way to the track the weather may be bright and sunny. Then, an hour before the start of the first race, clouds gather. Kaboom! Thunder, lightning and rain. Down comes the rain, soaking the track surface. When that happens, and I have no horses of my own running that day, it's back home for Sam Lewin. I've never been able to beat the mud. If you come across a good mud handicapper, let me know. I'll pinch him to see if he is real. I've heard people who claim to be expert in picking winners in the mud, but I've never met one who could prove it to my satisfaction.

There are five basic track conditions: fast, sloppy, good, frozen and muddy. Most track managements divide "muddy" into three categories—slow, muddy and heavy—with heavy being the worst. But those terms are merely variations on the same theme.

The *Morning Telegraph* and the *Daily Racing Form* provide some help to the bettor in dealing with various degrees of mud. Their past-performance charts carry "mud marks" after horses' names. An asterisk following a horse's name means he is classified as a fair mud runner. The symbox *x* means he is supposed to be good in the mud, and an *x* with a circle around it signifies a superior mud runner—usually a horse that has won in the mud.

My advice about mud, for what it's worth, is to disregard speed horses because they need firm footing to do their best running. Look instead for the plodders, horses that do not have early speed but do have a history of making up ground late in a race. In the mud, the tortoises win because the hares can't run.

The most formful type of track is the fast track. That is the kind on which all of my guidelines are meant to apply. Look for the same things on tracks classed as "sloppy" that you look for on a fast track. Sloppy tracks come when a brief, hard rain hits late in the program. Water collects on the surface but doesn't have a chance to soak in and make a track thick and holding. Water can make a track even faster than fast because the horses' hoofs can cut right through the water and surface material and strike the hard bottom underneath.

"Good" is a track condition I've always smiled at. It usually comes one or two sunny days after a heavy rain, when the track is mostly, but not quite, fully dry. The sun is shining, it's a fine day and the top of the track looks all right from the grandstand. The track may be wet underneath, but management doesn't want to spoil everyone's fun. Up goes the "good" sign.

On a day when the track really is good—dry on top but wet underneath—you can tack one second or so onto the horses' recent past running times. Late-running horses will rate a little more than their usual consideration on such days.

Often a track will change from good to fast during an afternoon. Then revert to your normal calculations. But if running times consistently are *more* than one second over the horses' usual form, look out. You are playing on a slow track, even if the sign says good. Unless you have more confidence in your ability in the mud than I do, you'd better go home early.

On "frozen" tracks—those which are very hard and slippery—you can throw out form. The best horse in a race usually doesn't win over a frozen surface. Some horses show a capability for handling frozen tracks, and you can look for an unusual number of repeat winners over the ice. Once a horse has won on a frozen track, he makes a good bet when he comes back on another.

God help horses that are sent out physically unsound to run on a frozen surface. No type of track is more conducive to injuries. Unfortunately, it appears that there will be more frozen-track racing in the years ahead, as more Northern tracks extend their seasons into the winter months.

To summarize:

1. If you must play in the mud, disregard speed horses and look for plodders, who run at a regular pace and make up ground late.

2. Fast tracks are the most formful; sloppy tracks can be even faster than fast.

3. When a track is good, tack one second onto horses' recent running times and give late runners more than their usual consideration.

4. Once a horse has won on a frozen track, he makes a good bet when he comes back on another.

First-timers

Very often you will encounter horses that have no recent form you can compare with that of the rest of the field. Leaving aside for the moment two-year-olds in their first races, these horses fall into three categories:

1) Horses that have come to the United States from other countries, 2) horses racing on a track for the first time during a meeting, and 3) horses returning to the races after a long period of inactivity.

Some bettors are inclined to stay away from these "first-timers" until they have established some current form. Sometimes this is a good idea and sometimes it isn't. If you make a principle of ignoring all such horses, you may pass up some good bets.

Horses just arriving in the United States from abroad are especially difficult to judge. The *Telegraph* and *Racing Form* carry the past performances of these horses, but the races will have been run on foreign tracks against competition with which you are unfamiliar. Unless a foreign horse's record is obviously good or bad, I suggest you wait a race or two to see how he performs in the U.S.

On the other hand, don't discriminate against foreign horses in your betting. My experience has shown that at all levels of competition they are as good or better than horses bred in the U.S. At the top stakes level, foreign horses won nine of the first sixteen runnings of the $150,000 Washington, D.C., International at Laurel. In the claiming races, I think horses from Europe and Latin America have a slight edge over our horses. Thoroughbred racing abroad isn't conducted on the wide scale that it is here. Less racing allows foreign breeders to be more selective than ours in bringing horses to the races.

How about horses racing on a track for the first time in a meeting against horses familiar with the surface? I add 5 lengths to the form of an animal that is appearing on a track for the first time; I look for a 5-length improvement the next time he runs.

All tracks are different and a horse needs at least one race to familiarize himself with an oval's surface and contours. A workout over the track may help in this familiarization process, but it is no substitute for an actual race. I add the 5 lengths to a horse's form even if he has worked out on the track.

The lone execption to my 5-length rule of thumb for "first-timers" is the top stakes horse that follows the big purses from track to track. Such horses—like Dr. Fager, Damascus and the filly Dark Mirage—are so good that they can beat the 5-length handicap. Against these horses, some edge might go to a horse that is familiar with a track, but not much. This is another instance of "class" overcoming obstacles.

Horses take vacations from racing for two reasons; injury and rest. When you see a horse in a race after an absence of two or three months, it's a good idea to try to determine why he was sent to the farm. If it was because of injury, take a close look at him when he comes out to run. This is a situation in which workout times can be of some value. If recent workouts have been very good, the horse is probably cured of whatever ailed him. If the workouts are very bad, he probably shouldn't be racing at all. If they are mediocre, take off the 5 lengths for a first-timer and be careful. Workouts also give some clues to the performance of a horse taken out of racing simply to rest without an injury being involved. Resting horses is a good practice that isn't followed widely enough these days. Horses, like people, need vacations. They usually feel better when they return.

Some trainers are very good at bringing horses up to winning form in their first pop out of the box. Old Max Hirsch of the

King Ranch is excellent in this regard. That is his style of train-ing. Other trainers who have much success with first-timers are Woody Stephens, Horatio Luro, Eddie Neloy, Jim Conway and H. A. Jerkens. Pay close attention to the horses these men bring to the races from the farm.

To summarize:

1. Unless a foreign horse is obviously good, wait until he establishes some form in this country before doing any serious betting on him. Nevertheless, don't discriminate against foreign horses in your betting.

2. A horse racing on a track for the first time is at a 5-length disadvantage against horses familiar with the surface. Top stakes horses are the exception to this rule.

3. Working clockings should be checked before you bet on a horse returning to the races after a long layoff.

On and Off the Turf

Turf, or grass, racing came to this country from Europe several decades ago and has since become enormously popular. Virtually every major race track now has a grass course, and puts it to use two or three times every racing day. For my money, turf racing is the best there is. I think the public agrees with me, and you'll see more turf racing in the years to come. It lends needed variety to a day at the track.

All of the guides that apply to main-track handicapping also apply on the turf. If anything, I believe that once you have made a few adjustments you'll find that turf racing is more formful than main-track racing. I think horses enjoy running on the grass, and that form is more likely to be true under those circumstances.

The main adjustment you will have to make on horses moving from the main, dirt track to the turf, and vice versa, is in running times. Using U.S. records as a rule, it seems that horses run slower on the turf than on dirt at distances through one mile; at about the same speed between 1$\frac{1}{16}$ miles and 1$\frac{1}{4}$ miles; and faster on the turf in the very long distances.

For example, at the end of 1967 the American record for 6 furlongs was 1:07$\frac{2}{5}$ on dirt and 1:09$\frac{2}{5}$ on turf. Thus you can expect a horse that has just run 6 furlongs on the turf to run that distance 2 seconds *faster* on the dirt track, and vice versa. At a mile, the adjustment should be about 1 second faster on the dirt than the turf. At 1$\frac{1}{2}$ miles, however, the U.S. turf-course record is more than 2 seconds faster than the dirst record. Thus, look for a slow-down in a horse coming from the turf to the main track at that distance, and a speed-up when the move is from the dirt to the turf.

There is a belief around the tracks that good mud horses are also good turf horses. I don't agree. Turf courses might appear to be slow, but they aren't. Many times the turf will be firmer than a fast main track.

Much more important is what happens to horses that show good speed in a turf-course race and come back to a fast main course within two weeks after their good turf effort. You'll see improvement in these horses that you won't believe. This is one "key" to the game I believe I have discovered; it has won many bets for me.

I think this "off-the-turf" improvement comes about because horses enjoy running on the grass so much. Horses are born and raised on farms and they do their first running in grassy pastures. I believe that a run on the grass awakens pleasant memories for many horses. Also, in turf races the trailing horses don't get dirt kicked at them, as on the main course. The thud-thud of the dirt against their bodies takes the heart out of some horses. A race that doesn't involve this unpleasantness seems to perk them up.

Finally, I think horses, like people, enjoy a little variety once in a while. A race over grass provides this variety. It's like taking your wife out to dinner—she'll feel better for days afterward because of the treat. Grass racing, I believe, does the same thing for horses.

A horse doesn't have to win on the grass to be a good bet when he comes back to the main course—he has only to show some measure of speed. I think the strongest combination comes when a horse runs well at $1\frac{1}{16}$ miles or $1\frac{1}{8}$ miles on the turf and then comes back to a $\frac{7}{8}$-mile race on the dirt course. The $\frac{7}{8}$-mile race is a long, hard sprint, and the longer race on the grass puts a horse in wonderful condition for this distance.

The same thing applies at other distances. Below is the past-performance chart of Bowler King as he went into a $\frac{3}{4}$-mile allowance race on the main course at Monmouth Park on June 10, 1968, only four days after a superb but losing grass effort over $\frac{5}{8}$ mile. (The circled "T" on the top line of the chart indicates the turf race.)

Notice Bowler King's last effort. He finished second by a nose in a race that was run in $57\frac{2}{5}$ seconds, equaling the turf-course record for the distance. Also notice his previous races. Bowler King usually ran well, but rarely won. In his nine previous starts he'd recorded only one first along with five seconds, two thirds and a sixth. His one win, which came on Oct. 5, 1967, was by a mere half-length in the fair time of $1:10\frac{2}{5}$ at $\frac{3}{4}$ mile.

Then Bowler King came off the turf, and look what happened! A 6-length win in the very good time of $1:09\frac{2}{5}$, only 1 second over the Monmouth track record. Bowler King in that race went off at odds of slightly better than 2–1, and he beat a 6–5 favorite, Irongate, who finished fourth after trying to run with Bowler

8th Monmouth

6 FURLONGS (Chute). (Decathlon, June 11, 1957, $108^{2/5}$, 4, 130.) Allowances. Purse $8,000. 4-years-olds and upward which have not won a race in 1968 other than maiden, claiming or starter. Weight, 122 lbs.. Non-winners of $6,500 twice since Sept. 30 allowed 3 lbs., $3,900 twice since Aug. 11, 5 lbs., $2,700 twice in 1967, 7 lbs., $2,400 twice in 1967, 10 lbs. (Maiden, claiming and starter races not considered.)

Bowler King*

B. h (1963–NJ), by Revoked–Toquila, by Equifox
Mrs. T.W. Baker, Jr. M.A. Buxton (Mrs. T.W. Baker, Jr.)

117

1968	5	0	2	3	$5,760
1967	15	3	6	2	$23,405

6Jun68–7Mth	fm 5f Ⓣ		$.45^{2/5}$	$.57^{2/5}$	Allowance	7	1	$3^{3\frac{1}{2}}$	3^{3}	$4^{2\frac{1}{2}}$	2no	HGrant	b 118	6.60	100—	Baitman 112no Bowler King 118^{nk} County Monaghan $117^{2\frac{1}{2}}$	Sharp	9
25May68–7GS	fst 6f	$.22^{3/5}$	$.46^{1/5}$	$1.10^{2/5}$	Allowance	4	1	2^{1}	$2^{1\frac{1}{2}}$	$2^{\frac{1}{2}}$	$3^{1\frac{1}{4}}$	JCulmone	b 116	2.70	91–19	Chicot 113^{nk} Ircngate 113^{1} Bowler King 116^{1}	Faltered stretch	8
8May68–8GS	fst 6f	$.21^{4/5}$	.45	$1.10^{2/5}$	Allowance	1	4	4^{2}	$2^{1\frac{1}{2}}$	$1^{\frac{1}{2}}$	2no	WBlum	b 113	d-2.30	92–16	Classic Work 113no d-Bowler King 113^{nk} Tornum 117^{1}	Bore out	8

8May68–d-Disqualified and placed third.

30Apr68–8GS	fst 6f	$.22^{3/5}$	$.46^{1/5}$	1.11	Allowance	6	2	2^{2}	$2^{1\frac{1}{2}}$	$3^{3\frac{1}{2}}$	3^{4}	WBlum	b 113	*1.30	85–18	On Your Mark II $113^{3\frac{1}{2}}$ Swoonland $113^{\frac{1}{2}}$ Bowler King 113^{h}	No excuse	7
23Apr68–7GS	fst 6f	.22	$.44^{3/5}$	$1.09^{1/5}$	Allowance	6	2	7^{2}	$2^{2\frac{1}{2}}$	2^{4}	2^{5}	WBlum	b 113	4.10	93–12	Country Friend 116^{5} Bowler King 113^{3} Spring Double $113^{\frac{3}{4}}$	Held on	8
18Nov67–TrP	fst 6f	$.22^{1/5}$	$.45^{1/5}$	$1.09^{4/5}$	Hurr'cneH	8	1	$3^{\frac{1}{2}}$	2^{h}	2^{h}	2^{4}	JVasquez	b 115	*1.00	85–17	Sir Winzalot 144^{4} Bowler King 115^{1} Breeze Maker 112^{2}	Gamely	8

18Nov67–The Hurricane Handicap run in two divisions –7th and 9th races.

14Oct67–6GS	fst 6f	$.22^{4/5}$	.46	1.11	Allowance	2	2	$3^{1\frac{1}{2}}$	$3^{1\frac{1}{2}}$	2^{h}	$2^{\frac{1}{2}}$	JCulmone	b 116	8.70	88–23	Jim J. $116^{\frac{1}{2}}$ Bowler King $116^{4\frac{1}{2}}$ Swoonaway 119^{nk}	Lost ground turn	7
5Oct67–5Atl	fst 6f	$.22^{1/5}$	$.45^{1/5}$	$1.10^{2/5}$	Allowance	4	2	$3^{2\frac{1}{2}}$	$3^{\frac{1}{2}}$	1^{h}	$1^{\frac{1}{2}}$	JCulmone	b 115	5.60	90–17	Bowler King $115^{\frac{1}{2}}$ Beaupy 115^{1} Lyrico $119^{\frac{1}{2}}$	Long, hard drive	6
23Aug67–6Sar	fst 7f	$.22^{3/5}$	$.45^{2/5}$	$1.22^{3/5}$	Allowance	7	1	$3^{3\frac{1}{2}}$	4^{5}	6^{8}	6^{12}	RTurcotte	b 117	5.70	85–11	Sun Gala 110^{h} Spring Double 124^{4} Wyoming Wildcat 115^{2}	Tired	8

LATEST WORKOUTS Jun 1 Mth 4f gd $.49^{3/5}$ b May 21 GS 5f fst 1.01 b May 16 GS 4f fst $.48^{3/5}$ h May 6 GS 3f sly .38 b

EIGHTH RACE

Mth — 34971

JUNE 10, 1968

6 FURLONGS (Chute). (Decathlon, June 11, 1957, 1.08⅖, 4, 130.) Allowances. Purse $8,000. 4—year-olds and upward which have not won a race in 1968 other than maiden, claiming or starter. Weight, 122 lbs. Non-winners of $6,500 twice since Sept. 30 allowed 3 lbs., $3,900 twice since Aug. 11, 5 lbs., $2,700 twice in 1967, 7 lbs., $2,400 twice in 1967, 10 lbs. (Maiden, claiming and starter races not considered.)

Value to winner $5,200, second $1,600, third $800, fourth $400. Mutuel pool $164,588.

Index	Horse	Eqt	A	Wt	PP	St	¼	½	Str	Fin	Jockey	Owner	Odds $1
34943Mth²	—Bowler King	b	5	117	1	3	3ʰ	2ʰ	1½	1⁶	J Culmone	Mrs—T W Baker Jr.	2.10
33297Lrl⁷	—Flower's Boy	b	5	117	4	7	7	7	4¹	2ⁿᵏ	J Velasquez	A J O'Connell	11.10
34687Aqu²	—GoldenButtons	b	5	113	5	5	6½	6ʰ	5½	3¾	W Gavidia	Ada L. Rice	5.80
34769GS²	—Irongate		5	118	7	1	1¹	1ʰ	2¹	4²½	H Grant	Miss Mary V. Fisher	1.20
34805GS⁵	—Night Cloud	b	5	112	6	2	2½	3³	3ʰ	5ⁿᵏ	P Kallai	Narudson Stable	11.30
34353GS⁵	—Trish M.	b	5	117	2	6	5³	5½	6²	6¹½	C Baltazar	Charfran Stable	14.10
33216Aqu⁶	—Twin Teddy	b	7	117	3	4	4¹½	4ʰ	7	7	M Miceli	Miss C Morabito	32.70

Time .22⅕, .45, 1.09⅖. Track fast.

$2 Mutuel Prices:

1—BOWLER KING	6.20	3.80	3.00
4—FLOWER'S BOY		7.20	3.80
5—GOLDEN BUTTONS			4.00

B. h, by Revoked—Toquila, by Equifox. Trainer M. A. Buston. Bred by Mrs. T. W. Baker, Jr. (N.J.).

IN GATE AT 5.24. OFF AT 5.24 EASTERN DAYLIGHT TIME. Start good. Won ridden out.

BOWLER KING, outside rivals from the start, gained command after settling for the drive and drew out under intermittent pressure. FLOWER'S BOY, slow to gain best stride, rallied between horses to loom a factor in upper stretch and faltered. GOLDEN BUTTONS came wide for the drive and lacked the needed late response. IRONGATE sprinted clear at the start, saved ground and faltered. NIGHT CLOUD was sent between horses to reach even terms for the lead entering the stretch and tired from his efforts. TWIN TEDDY was through early.

King in the early going. I cashed a nice bet on good old Bowler King that day.

One word of caution. This off-the-turf improvement usually doesn't come if the dirt track isn't fast. Also, if more than two weeks elapse between a horse's good turf showing and his main-course race, the edge is often lost and the improvement won't show up. Within those limitations, horses coming off good turf efforts make wonderful bets. You'll find a few good longshots this way.

To summarize:

1. Horses run faster on the dirt than on turf at distances through 1 mile; at about the same speed between $1\frac{1}{16}$ miles and $1\frac{1}{4}$ miles; and faster on the turf thereafter. Adjust running times accordingly when horses move from the turf to the main track, and vice versa.

2. Don't believe the old line that good mud horses are necessarily good turf horses.

3. Horses that show good speed on the turf will often show marked improvement if they are raced on a fast main track within two weeks after their strong turf effort. Be especially alert for these horses.

Longshots

A lot of people come to the track for the sole purpose of finding a good longshot. More often than not, they go home disappointed. Winning longshots don't jump out of the newspaper charts screaming, "Here I am!" Good longshots—those with a fair chance of winning—are hard to find.

To improve your chance of finding good longshots, I suggest

that you do your prerace analyzing without referring to morning-line odds. In this way, you won't be influenced by the track handicapper's opinion of the horses. The same goes for news-papers and tip-sheet selectors. You might want to check your calculations with theirs, but only after you have made your own choices. This will protect you from being prejudiced against horses the professional selectors don't like.

As I've said, you should be alert for "overlays" in the betting. Overlays are horses that don't get the public backing they de-serve and thus go off at higher odds than they should. Be careful in betting on this kind of horse. It might have been an injury that forced up the odds. But stay alert for them anyway.

True overlays are quite rare. Usually, the best you can hope for are a few indications that a longshot *might* stand a good chance in a race. Below is the chart of Final Lap, a colt who won his first race in 24 starts on June 10, 1968, at Monmouth Park (his winning race is shown on the top line of his chart). His odds in that race were slightly better than 20–1.

What was there about Final Lap's past performance that might have alerted you that he was about to come up with a good one? First, you'll notice that his winning race was at $1\frac{1}{16}$ miles on the turf, while in his previous race, over the turf at 1 mile, he had moved up from tenth at the quarter-mile mark to fourth at the finish. He wound up 12 lengths behind the winner, but he did pass some horses toward the end. The extra $\frac{1}{16}$ mile apparently gave him the added distance he needed to catch the leaders. Also notice that Final Lap ran for a $9,000 claiming tag in his winning race, down from $11,000 in the race before. Although I don't lean toward horses dropping in price after running a mediocre race, it appears that the drop helped Final Lap.

You'll see that on May 14, 1968, at Garden State Park in New Jersey (initials "GS" on the table), Final Lap was the even-money

Final Lap **$12,000** **Dk. b. or br. c (1965–Ky), by The Irishman–Stretch Drive, by Bimelech**

T. Titone H. Napoli (Wheatley Stable)

117

1968	16	1	1	0	$4,840
1967	8	M	0	1	$615

10Jun68–9Mth	fm*	$1\frac{1}{16}$	Ⓣ		1.14	$1.47\frac{4}{5}$	Clm	9000	8	8	$8^{9\frac14}$	$5^{6\frac12}$	$4^{\frac34}$	$1^{1\frac14}$	VTejada	b113	20.10	–	Final Lap $113^{1\frac14}$ Naughty Joke 115^{h} Wild Fella $115^{2\frac12}$	Brisk drive	9
3Jun68–7Mth	gd	1	Ⓣ		$.48\frac{4}{5}$	$1.41\frac{2}{5}$	Clm	11000	9	10	10^{11}	$9^{4\frac34}$	$7^{8\frac14}$	4^{12}	DHidalgo	b115	36.20	63–25	Not Too Modest 117^{nk} Bungalow 110^{7} Creative $114^{4\frac12}$	Slow early	11
25May68–5GS	gd	$1\frac{1}{16}$		.47	$1.12\frac{4}{5}$	1.47	Md Sp Wt		2	8	7^{14}	$6^{8\frac14}$	$7^{4\frac14}$	$5^{6\frac34}$	BThornburg	b115	15.10	63–19	Please Behave 115^{nk} Mertensia $114^{4\frac12}$ Burnt Sand 115^{2}	Slow early	10
14May68–4GS	fst	1^{70}		$.47\frac{3}{5}$	$1.13\frac{2}{5}$	$1.44\frac{2}{5}$	Md	7500	1	4	4^{4}	$2^{1\frac12}$	2^{h}	2^{nk}	BThornburg	b115	*1.00	72–18	Hip Check 113^{nk} Final Lap 115^{10} Noble Sid 113^{6}	Couldn't reach win'r	6
8May68–1GS	fst	6f		$.22\frac{2}{5}$	.46	$1.12\frac{1}{5}$	Md	7500	11	2	8^{6}	$7^{8\frac12}$	$8^{7\frac12}$	5^{3}	BThornburg	116	3.80	80–16	Old Watts 116no Tote The Mail $117^{2\frac12}$ Happy Medium $109^{\frac12}$	Mild bid	12
26Apr68–2GS	fst	6f		$.22\frac{2}{5}$	$.46\frac{3}{5}$	$1.13\frac{1}{5}$	Md	10000	1	9	$9^{8\frac14}$	$9^{9\frac34}$	$8^{5\frac12}$	$6^{2\frac34}$	BThornburg	115	13.60	75–18	Trueno $115^{\frac12}$ Winter Man $113^{1\frac12}$ Roulette Queen 113^{h}	No mishap	10
11Apr68–8GP	fm*	1	Ⓣ			$1.38\frac{1}{5}$	Clm	14000	10	9	$9^{6\frac14}$	7^{8}	$7^{3\frac14}$	$6^{9\frac12}$	BThornburg	b116	38.80	–	Energetic 112no Slicky Jim $118^{1\frac12}$ Swimmin' Hole $116^{1\frac12}$	No factor	12
28Mar68–6GP	fm	1	Ⓣ		$.46\frac{3}{5}$	$1.36\frac{1}{5}$	Clm	16000	2	11	10^{11}	9^{11}	$8^{9\frac12}$	7^{11}	GGallitano[5]	111	65.90	81– 8	Pit Stop $111^{\frac34}$ Relentless Pursuit $112^{\frac12}$ Sir Omni $116^{1\frac14}$	No speed	11
20Mar68–7GP	fm	1	Ⓣ		$.46\frac{4}{5}$	1.38	Allowance		8	10	10^{14}	11^{15}	9^{14}	$7^{7\frac12}$	DWalkers[5]	109	60.00	75–13	Dilettante 104^{1} Lady Carene $109^{\frac12}$ Restless Brook $114^{\frac12}$	Slow start	12
14Mar68–8GP	fm	$1\frac{1}{16}$	Ⓣ			$1.43\frac{1}{5}$	Allowance		4	8	7^{11}	$7^{7\frac14}$	7^{14}	7^{11}	RWholey Jr[5]	108	91.40	77–13	Go Marching $115^{2\frac12}$ Urbane Charm $122^{\frac12}$ Lady Carene 113^{3}	No speed	9

LATEST WORKOUTS May 23 GS 5f fst 1.03 b May 5 GS 3f fst $.37\frac{2}{5}$ b Apr 30 GS 5f fst 1.05 b

favorite in a $7,500 claiming race. (The little star next to his odds means he was favored.) This indicates that the bettors saw *something* in this horse once before. I admit that isn't much to go on, but as I said, longshots don't shout at you.

What made Final Lap win that one race was that he was a come-from-behind horse in a field that included several speed horses. The speed horses tired one another out and allowed Final Lap to slip past them. Pace made the race for Final Lap; he finally found a race that was run to his liking.

To summarize:

1. To improve your chances of finding good longshots, do your prerace handicapping without referring to professional handicappers' selections or morning-line odds.

2. Be alert for betting overlays that apparently aren't caused by an injury to the overlaid horse.

3. Look for little things in a longshot's past performances, such as races in which he showed early speed or gained late ground but didn't win, races in which he went off at low odds and (in claiming races) changes in his claiming price. Mostly, look for a pace that might finally suit a longshot.

5

The Long and Short of It

Determining pace is the main objective of my style of handicapping, and the crucial factor in determining the likely pace of a race is the length at which it is run. "Distance" races—those of 1 mile and above—must be analyzed differently than sprint races. The size and contour of the track, the weights the horses carry, the importance of post position and the strategy of the jockeys all must be considered in relation to the distance of ground the horses are assigned to cover. We've already touched on some of these relationships. Now we shall look at them in greater detail.

⅜ Mile

Remember what I said about the need to be flexible in your handicapping? Well, in ⅜-mile races—the "baby" races run for brand-new two-year-olds at Hialeah, Santa Anita and a few other tracks—most of the guides I've already given you go right out the window.

There is no pace in a ⅜-mile race; it is the 100-yard dash of horse racing. Three-eighths-mile races are run on straightaways, so post position normally plays no role. On top of this, you must be a close student of workouts and an odds-board watcher to get the most out of two-year-olds running this shortest of thoroughbred sprints.

I advise close attention to two-year-olds' workouts because young colts and fillies are very consistent animals. You might not expect them to be, but they are. Two-year-olds, I suppose, are like most youngsters starting out in their work. They are ready to go and full of enthusiasm every day. It's only when going to the races becomes a regular chore that horses develop the laziness and inconsistencies that typically mark their later careers.

The two-year-old is the most consistent of all horses during the first half-dozen races of his career. Once having established a running time at ⅜ mile in a race or workout, the young colt or filly almost always proceeds to equal or better that time. That is the nature of the beast.

Often, two-year-olds stage their prerace workouts at training tracks or other places that aren't open to the public. Thus, their times won't be a matter of public record. This is where odds-board watching comes in. *You* might not know how good each two-year-old is, but well-informed regular bettors will. Frequently they will help establish the proper animal as the favorite. In my observation, a higher proportion of favorites win two-year-old races at ⅜ mile than any other kind of race. By following the favorites, you will find yourself taking short prices on many two-year-olds in the "dash." But you will also have more than the usual 33 percent chance of seeing the favorite win.

Some jockeys have proved themselves to be excellent riders of two-year-olds in their first starts. Among them are Ray Broussard, Jimmy Nichols, Elden Coffman, Johnny Rotz and Bob Ussery. These riders have a knack of getting their mounts out of the gate quickly and in good style. This is known as "post alertness." The start is all-important in the ⅜-mile race. A surprising number of horses win the dash from the second or third position with ⅛ mile to go, but very few can win it from far off the lead. There simply isn't enough distance for a late runner to make a proper bid at ⅜ mile.

The jockeys who have success with two-year-olds in this event are usually those who don't rely heavily on the whip in their riding. Many states don't allow whips to be used on horses of this age. Since two-year-olds have a habit of veering all over the track when they run, it is thought that the use of the whip might make them run even more erratically. If you bet at a track where ⅜-mile baby races are run, you should look for jockeys who have shown they can win without the whip.

Another point to watch for in this race is the way shadows strike the track. Most race-track grandstands face away from the sun, so that in the late afternoon the shadow of the grandstand will fall across the outside portion of the track. On humid, sunny days, or after a rain, this will often mean that the shaded outside portion of the track will be softer than the inside, where the sun is beating down steadily. Horses tend to bunch around the rail in races around a turn, so the sun-shadow factor usually won't be important. But it can come into play on ⅜-mile races run down a straightaway in front of the grandstand, where the outside is more heavily used. The advantage, naturally, is with horses in the sunny, inside post positions.

A hedge alongside part of the track on which this race is run can produce the same sun-shadow effect as the shadow of the grandstand. The area of the track that the hedge shades is likely to be softer than the portion fully exposed to the sun. Give a *slight* edge to horses starting on the sunny side of the track.

A point of caution on the sun-shade factor: It should not be given too much importance and should come into play only in deciding between very evenly matched horses.

The study of breeding will help the bettor find winners among two-year-olds running at any distance, but that subject is far too complicated to deal with in a book of this sort. Serious racing fans can pursue the study of breeding on their own. Several manuals that list the breeding records of various stables, breeding farms and individual stallions and mares are issued annually. I highly recommend this study.

To summarize:

1. There is no pace in a ⅜-mile race and post position normally plays no role.

2. Pay attention to workouts and the odds-board. Two-year-olds who run the ⅜ mile are very consistent; once having established a clocking at the distance, they will usually equal or better it.

3. A high proportion of favorites win in this race.

4. Jockeys who get their mounts out of the gate quickly and show they can win without relying on the whip do well in ⅜-mile races.

5. Watch for the sun-shadow factor, but use it sparingly.

⅝ Mile

Originally, ⅝-mile races were run mainly for two-year-olds, but lately tracks have added more events over this distance for older horses. The ⅝-mile race has become a favorite of trainers who want to get the most out of the sprint potential of horses in their barns.

Many two-year-olds begin their careers running the ⅝ mile instead of the ⅜. This is something that I favor strongly both as a horse-owner and stable manager. Once a two-year-old has become accustomed to running the ⅜-mile dash on the straight-away, he has to be retaught to negotiate the turn that is involved in the ⅝-mile race. Since all of a horse's future races will be run around turns, I believe it is best for him to start out in races where a turn is a factor. As a bettor, I think that two-year-olds that make their debuts at ⅝ mile usually do better than the others at the longer distances they run later in their first year on the tracks and afterward.

Post position plays a bigger part in the ⅝-mile race than in any other distance. Over the ⅝, the run into the first turn invariably is short. This gives a strong edge to horses starting from the inside positions, no matter what their running style. Late-running horses that start from the outside are at an extreme disadvantage going ⅝ mile. The whole pack is between them and the rail, and they will have to cover much extra ground to get themselves into any kind of contending position. It takes a hell of a horse to beat that handicap.

On paper it might appear that speed horses would have the best of it in the ⅝-mile sprint. But I've observed that speed fails in many, many cases over this distance. The reason is simple. There is an overabundance of speed in the majority of ⅝-mile races. Every trainer at a meeting with a front-running horse in his barn shoots for the ⅝-mile races. At the ¾-mile distances and above, you might find two or three speed horses in a race. At ⅝, there may be five or six such horses. The result often is a furious early pace and a late-running winner.

Key fractional times to look for in handicapping ⅝-mile races are the 22-second quarter-mile and the 45-second half-mile. When you can locate only one horse in a race that can hit those fractions, he is your bet. He will likely have a commanding lead at the head of the stretch and the rest of the field will have a tough time catching him. If two or more horses have similar times for the quarter- and half-miles, look for a horse that can win from just off the pace. It takes courage to bet on a late-running horse in the ⅝-mile sprint, but many times you will be rewarded with long-priced winners. A good standard finishing time for the best horses in the ⅝ mile is 59 seconds. If your prerace analysis indicates a sizzling early pace, look for a fast finisher that has shown he can go the distance in around that time.

A word of caution is in order about evaluating the chances of a two-year-old's moving from the ⅜-mile to the ⅝-mile race. Many times young colts and fillies will post exceptionally fast times over the ⅜-mile distance and then become big disappointments going ⅝ mile. This is because they encounter trouble in negotiating the turn, or because they are ⅜-mile horses and nothing more. As I have said, two-year-olds are very consistent animals. Their consistency will carry over to the ⅝-mile distance. However, it is best to wait until they have established their form over the longer distance before doing any serious betting on them.

To summarize:

1. Horses with inside positions have a big advantage in ⅝-mile races.

2. It's a short sprint, but don't neglect the late runners, especially when there is an overabundance of early speed in a field.
3. Key fractional times to watch for are 22 seconds for the quarter-mile and 45 seconds for the half-mile. A good final time is 59 seconds.
4. Wait until two-year-olds show they can handle a turn before betting on them seriously at ⅝ mile.

¾ Mile

The most popular distance at the race track is ¾ mile, or 6 furlongs. Trainers prepare their horses mainly to run this distance. It is a sprint race, so it attracts speed horses. Trainers of come-from-behind horses who fail at ⅝ mile like the distance because they think the extra ⅛ mile will give their horses a chance to win. It is a distance that bettors face several times a day at most tracks.

The pace of the ¾-mile race is much like that of the ⅝. Winners come from on or off the pace depending on how the first half-mile of the race is run. Fractional times to watch for in this race are slightly slower than the key times in the ⅝ mile. Look for speed horses that can run the first quarter-mile in better than 22⅖ seconds and the half in better than 45⅖ seconds. If one horse alone can beat those fractions, he's a good bet. If two or three horses have shown they can run the half-mile in 45⅖ seconds or better, the actual pace is likely to be faster than that, and the winner probably will come from somewhere off the pace. A good final time for better horses in the ¾ mile is 1:10⅗.

Horses need more staying power to run the ¾ mile sucessfully than for the ⅝ mile. Some sprinters tend to "stop" running in

¾-mile races; the final ⅛ mile kills them. If you favor a horse that likes to run in the lead, make sure he can go that last ⅛ mile.

Be on the alert for horses who make up ground late in ⅝-mile races, but not quite enough to win. The extra ⅛ mile in the ¾ race might give them the distance they need to finish on top. Beware of horses that lead but stop going distances longer than ¾ mile. The early pace in the ¾ is usually faster than that of longer races, and the horse that leads and stops at, say, 1¹⁄₁₆ mile probably will never see the lead at all in the ¾-mile race.

Post position is important in this race, but not quite as important as it is at the ⅝-mile distance. The extra ⅛ mile is usually added at the portion of the track where the race starts, so the run into the first turn is longer than at ⅝ and horses have more room to maneuver. Inside post positions should still be favored for horses of all styles.

When ¾-mile races are started out of a chute, watch again for hedges near the starting gate. Such a hedge will cast its shadow on the inside of the track in the first few yards. On humid days, or after a rain, it's likely that the early going in post positions 1 and 2 might be a little sticky. This would subtract something from the inside post advantage.

Weight becomes a factor in this race. As I've said, a weight advantage won't make a poor horse beat a good one, no matter how great that advantage. Nevertheless, begin paying attention to weight differences between horses that otherwise appear to be evenly matched.

To summarize:

1. Inside post positions have an edge in the ¾ mile, but not as great as in the ⅝.

2. Speed still rules at this distance, but staying power also

plays a role. Horses that finish with a rush at ⅝ mile can win here. Beware of horses that lead but stop at longer distances; they might not see the lead in the faster-paced ¾-mile race.

3. Key fractional times to watch for are 22⅖ seconds for the quarter and 45⅖ for the half. Better horses finish in 1:10⅗ or thereabouts.

4. Watch for hedges near the starting gate after a rain.

5. Begin paying attention to weight.

⅞ Mile

The ⅞-mile race is run at only about a dozen major tracks, and it almost always begins in a chute set off the main course. Many racing people think the 1½-mile race is the most trying distance for horses to run, but I think the ⅞ mile is the most difficult. It is a long, long sprint that must be run all-out all the way. At the same time, I think that the ⅞ distance is the most "formful" of all races. By that I mean it is the distance at which there will be fewest fluke winners. The best horse will win many more times than not.

The most important factor in handicapping a ⅞-mile race is the very long run into the first turn. In this race, horses run about ⅜ of a mile before they hit the turn. This should have a big influence on the way you evaluate post position and fractional times.

On post position, my maxim in ⅞-mile races is: Speed horses from the outside, late runners from the inside. Late-runners always do best starting from the inside because it makes it easier for them to save ground along the rail. For speed horses, however, an outside post position provides a clear path from which to shoot past the field and settle into the rail for the final drive. If a horse starting from the outside has good early speed, he won't get caught on the edge of the pack on the turn as he might in the ⅝ mile or even the ¾. Inside speed horses are more likely to encounter interference as they try for the lead.

Because of the long, straight start of the ⅞-mile race, fractional times will be similar to the ¾-mile standards even though the distance is longer. Good fractional standards for speed horses at ⅞ are 23 seconds flat at the quarter and 45⅗ at the half. A good final racing time is 1:22.

Don't expect any faint-hearted sprinters to win ⅞-mile races. Speed horses are likely to be challenged at several points during the race and they must be able to withstand each challenge if they are to win from on the pace. Think long and hard before you bet on a horse whose record shows that he hangs on to win ¾-mile races by less than 2 lengths; he'll likely get caught. Look instead for horses that win ¾-mile races by substantial margins. If the latter type of horse shows you those 23 and 45⅗ fractions and holds up well for the last quarter, he'll likely hang on to win the ⅞ mile.

Give a little more importance to weight in the ⅞ mile than you would in the ¾, but don't make it too important.

To summarize:

1. Speed horses do best from outside post positions; late runners do best from the inside.

2. Discount faint-hearted sprinters. Look for strong sprinters or horses which close fast but don't quite make it in the ¾ mile.

3. Good fractional times are 23 seconds and 45⅗. A good finishing time is 1:22.

Mile and Up

The 1-mile race is where the sprints end and the distance events begin. A few tracks—Aqueduct and Belmont in New York and Arlington Park in Chicago—run mile races from a chute around only one turn. There you should treat the mile just as you would treat the ⅞ mile, but be even more careful that your speed horse doesn't quit in the late running. At most tracks, however, races beginning with the mile are run around two turns. Two turns are what separate the sprints from the the distance races in race-track parlance.

Most major dirt race tracks are 1 mile in circumference, measured along the inside rail. Turf courses are somewhat shorter, because they are usually placed inside the main tracks. Longer races over the turf sometimes begin from chutes that begin in the infield and turn slightly into the turf course. This bend gives a slight edge to inside horses.

The distance into the first turn plays a major part in the way you should analyze races of 1 mile and up. In mile races on mile tracks, the run into the first turn is usually short and an advantage should go to the inside post positions. The post advantage diminishes as the start of the race is moved farther from the first turn.

At races of 1⅛ miles or more, post positions usually mean little because the race is long enough for each horse eventually to reach the running position that best suits his style. The extra strides required of outside-post-position horses in long races aren't as important as they are in the sprints, where every step is magnified.

Weight becomes an important part of your calculations when you encounter races beginning with one mile. The "five pounds equals a length rule" should be applied at the mile within the limits I've already mentioned. At 1¼ and 1½ miles, five pounds should equal 2 or 3 lengths when you are comparing horses of fairly equal ability.

Standard final running time for good horses running a mile is 1:35. Fractional times to look for are 24 seconds at the quarter, 47 seconds at the half and 1:11 at the three-quarters. Remember, those times are meant to apply to good horses. Claiming-race horses will show you what times to expect from them by their past performances.

Standard final time for 1¹⁄₁₆ miles is 1:44. For 1⅛ miles, anything under 1:50 is very good; the best stakes horses can go the distance in less than 1:48. A good standard time for 1¼ miles is between 2:02 and 2:03; this race, the Kentucky Derby distance, is seldom run by horses of the claiming class. At 1½ miles, which is run only in a few stakes events, anything between 2:28 and 2:30 is good.

It's natural to suppose that come-from-behind horses deserve the most consideration in the distance races, but this isn't necessarily the case. As a random illustration, two of the three races run at 1 mile or more at Aqueduct in New York on July 13, 1968, were won by horses that led all the way. The third distance race that day, the 1¼ $75,000 Dwyer Handicap, was won by Stage Door Johnny, who was fourth, 3½ lengths from the lead, after a half-mile. He took the lead at the top of the homestretch and breezed home 2 lengths ahead.

As in the sprints, your prerace analysis of the distance events should center on the manner in which the early portions of the race figure to be run. To be sure, the added distance will give a better chance to horses that pick up ground in the closing phases of races of less than a mile but still fall short at the wire. But often, sprinters who "stop" in the ¾ or ⅞ because they are pressed,

pressed, pressed, find that their speed in a slow-paced distance event puts them so far in the lead that they cannot be caught. A horse that shows he can open a lead of a half-dozen lengths at the half-mile mark of a long race always deserves a lot of consideration.

The 1968 Bowling Green Handicap, run at 1½ miles over the turf at Belmont Park was such a race. The favorite, High Hat, the top-weighted horse in the race, opened an 8-length lead at the half-mile mark. He was caught at the top of the stretch but the effort required of his pursuers to overcome his wide early lead allowed him to hang on and get his nose under the wire first. Even races of the longest distance can be "stolen" by a horse with great early speed.

The Challenge of the Distance Race

Distance races present a special challenge to the handicapper because of the complexity of the figuring involved. Unlike the sprints, which seem to be over almost as soon as they begin, much skill is needed to analyze the probable course of races run at 1 mile and over. Horses in such races can and sometimes do come on to win from more than a dozen lengths off the pace. And as I've just mentioned, the possibility always exists that a speed horse will steal a long race with a strong early burst. The "plodder," the steady-running horse that stands little chance in the sprints, must also be taken into consideration over a long distance, especially if your analysis indicates that a fast-paced race will produce some very tired horses in the final quarter-mile.

Racing fans love the distance events because they offer a chance to see the horses run by the grandstand twice. Many trainers, however, dislike such races because of what they take out of their animals physically and the difficulty of training horses to go long distances. For a track's management, the scheduling of distance events represents a tug-of-war between the wishes of the fans and those of the trainers and owners.

Unfortunately for the fans, I think we will see fewer distance events in the years to come. Track managements today are under increasing pressures from their stockholders and from state governments to take in more dollars by running more races and by extending racing seasons. More races will increase the physical stress on the horses. Under those conditions, I think it is inevitable that, except for a few traditional stakes events, distance races will be run less frequently in the future.

To summarize:

1. Weight begins to play a role at 1 mile; the longer the race the more important weight becomes.

2. At 1⅛ miles and over, post position plays a minor role. Between 1 and 1⅛ miles, the length of the run into the first turn determines the importance of post position (the shorter the run, the more important post position becomes).

3. Late runners have a better chance of winning distance races than they do sprints, but races of any length can be stolen by a strong display of early speed. Sprinters who "stop" at distances of less than 1 mile because they are challenged sometimes can gain big leads and win distance events.

4. Good standard finishing times are 1:35 for the mile, 1:44 for 1⅟₁₆ miles, 1:50 for 1⅛ miles, 2:02 to 2:03 for 1¼ miles and 2:28 to 2:30 for 1½ miles.

Horses Have Names

Your prerace study shouldn't end when you fold your newspaper and head for the track. What you see at the track is almost as important in determining your bets as what you read in the horses' past-performance listings. Observation is a very important element in my style of handicapping. The horseplayer who is a good observer—who knows what to look for and when—will have an important advantage over his less observant fellow fans.

A good pair of binoculars is a necessity for a day at the track. If you don't own a pair, you may rent one for the day at the concession stands that many tracks have. If you watch the races from the clubhouse or the grandstand, as most fans do, you will need binoculars just to watch the horses come out on the track for the races. Even if you are one of those sun-worshipers who line up alongside the outer rail, you'll need the glasses to get a good look at the races themselves. Make it your business to sit or stand where you'll have an unobstructed view of the proceedings.

Being a good observer requires will power. At just about every track the odds-board is the most eye-catching feature. The lights flash on and off, the odds change and all sorts of messages ("Welcome to the Hackensack Elks") are flashed. It's practically hypnotic. It provides just about the only "action" during those long delays between races which too many track managements have made part of the racing scene. Nevertheless, you'll have to learn to tear your eyes away from the odds board. In the early days, when I went to the tracks with Fatty Anderson, I had a lot of trouble doing this. I'd sit there watching the board while Fatty would have his binoculars trained on the animals warming up for the next race. One day Fatty asked why I wasn't watching the horses.

"How do you expect me to find overlays to bet if I don't watch the board?" I said.

"You'll find more overlays under those jockeys down there than on that big pinball machine in the infield," he answered. As usual, Fatty was right.

You'll need more will power to fight off the horseplayer's natural tendency to watch only his own horse during the running of a race, but that too is a necessity. Watch the whole race as it develops, paying special attention to the action that starts at the pole ⅜ mile from the finish. The ⅜ pole is the crucial point in most races. That is where the lead horse will show if he can hang on to win and where the come-from-behinders make their serious challenges. If the horse you bet on is in contention at this point, you won't have to worry about seeing him.

In watching the whole race you will see things that will help in your future betting. In about 90 percent of all races, one horse or more will encounter some fairly serious interference, since horses inevitably get in one another's way as they fight for position. For instance, you might see a horse being boxed-in along the railing early and not get free in time to challenge the leaders. He'll make a late run, but fall short. The next time this horse runs, his past-performance chart will only show that he placed fourth or fifth, or whatever his position was, and that he was so many lengths behind the winner. On paper it will look as though he threw in a bad race, but you will know otherwise from having watched him. That knowledge will give you a nice edge on the rest of the public and you might stand to cash in on some high odds.

For the same reason, you shouldn't go home early from a day at the track. Stay and watch the last few races, even if you don't plan to bet on them. You can never tell when something you see will be a help in the future. There is no substitute for watching horses run in competition.

Your observation of the horses should begin well before race time. It's a good idea to visit the paddock before each race. Besides adding color to your day at the track, it will give you a chance to see the horses close up. If you can't make it to the paddock, be ready with your binoculars when the horses step onto the track.

The first characteristic people notice about horses is their color.

Discard this factor immediately from any betting calculations. Color has no effect on the way a horse runs. Chestnut, brown, mahogany, black or gray—they're all the same as far as winning goes.

Size of the Horse

Probably the next thing to be noticed is the comparative size of the various horses. Here there is room for argument. Many trainers lean strongly toward big, strong-looking horses as the best runners, but among male horses, at least, I have no size preference. For every good, large colt or horse (a colt becomes a horse and a filly becomes a mare at age five) you can name, I can name a good small one. For illustration, take some recent Kentucky Derbys. In 1962, Decidedly, a small horse, beat big Ridan. In 1963, the winner was Chateaugay; Candy Spots, one of the biggest horses ever to run in the Derby, finished third. In 1964, smallish Northern Dancer won out over the ponderous Hill Rise. I'm not saying a small colt will usually beat a big one, but if he can run his size won't hurt.

Fillies

When it comes to fillies and mares, however, I definitely prefer them small. Female horses very rarely beat males—that's why they get weight advantages when they run in "mixed" races. But once in a while a great big "amazon" filly or mare will come out to face the boys and because of her size she will pick up betting support. If you want to fight history, and you think that *based on her record* a female horse has a chance to win in a "mixed" race, go ahead and bet on her. But don't be fooled by the size of the "amazon" filly.

There have been some good big fillies—Hirsch Jacobs' Priceless Gem was one—but on the whole I think small fillies have been more successful. There's no better example of this than the top three-year-old filly of 1968, Dark Mirage. This filly weighed only 710 pounds (average weight for three-year-old fillies is between 800 and 900 pounds and three-year-old colts average about 1,000 pounds), but she won the Coaching Club American Oaks stakes; the Acorn and the Mother Goose—the filly "Triple Crown." In the American Oaks at Belmont, she won by an amazing 12 lengths. She skips over the ground very nicely, as do all good little fillies.

My performance for small female horses extends to the way they perform as brood mares. They seem to take to the sexual relationship better than big mares, and they seem to make better mothers. That's been my observation.

Smaller horses generally have an advantage over large horses in the important area of physical condition. Thoroughbreds' bodies are too large for their legs, and that's where the vast majority of racing ailments occur. Small horses put a lot less strain on their legs than large ones, and thus are less susceptible to injury. For the same reason, small horses seem to recover faster from their ailments. Because I strongly favor sound horses over those with physical problems, I wind up betting on smaller horses more often than on large ones.

Age

The age of a thoroughbred has a bearing on his speed. Colts and fillies typically begin racing as two-year-olds. Unless they prove worthless as racers or serious injury intervenes, they usually can continue to race until the age of eight or nine. A few, but only a few, race after that. The oldest horse to win a race in 1967 was Be Fly, a fourteen-year-old. He also finished second four times and third once in eighteen starts. Quite an animal, but unusual.

Most horses reach their peak of speed and strength as five-year-olds. After that they begin to decline. With today's hard racing and the very high fees being paid to owners who want to put their horses into breeding, fewer and fewer top horses race much past their fifth year. This, I believe, is racing's loss. Kelso, a gelding who thus had no stud value, won big races into his eighth year. Other horses could do the same if their owners would let them.

Two- and three-year-old horses race mostly in their own age groups. The top early-year stakes for three-year-olds are run with the horses carrying equal weight. Colts and fillies graduate into the handicap class later in their three-year-old year. In handicap races the track's racing secretary attempts to equalize competition by assigning the most weight to the horse he considers the best. Some animals can't or won't make that jump. Man O' War, considered by some to be the greatest horse ever, quit racing after the age of three because of the crushing weights that racing secretaries heaped on him in handicap events. He won one race carrying 138 pounds, two pounds less than the theoretical top weight a thoroughbred can carry.

Placed against older horses, three-year-olds usually are at some disadvantage, although their past performances can be relied upon to tell you whether they measure up to their competition. Similarly, horses over six years old are usually at some disadvantage racing in younger company. However, I believe that recent past performances should take precedence over birth dates.

Sex of the Horse

The sex of the animals is another factor the bettor should take into consideration. As I've already indicated, one of the most consistent facts of racing is that male horses of any age usually beat females. Enough said.

Within the general class of male horses, however, there are three sex categories. The first, of course, is the fully sexed colt or horse. Second is the gelding, a male that has been unsexed. The third type, variously described as the "mono," "crypto" or "ridgling," is a male of any age with one (sometimes both) reproductive organs missing from the sac. The ridgling is a fairly rare animal, one you won't encounter too often in your betting. When one does appear, he will be so designated in the program. I've had some experience with animals of this type and typically they are more inconsistent than colts or geldings. They tend to sulk. I believe they are bothered by the one testicle that isn't in the right place.

Depending on the way he develops, a ridgling will be operated on to make him a true colt or a gelding. When that happens, he usually becomes a more consistent runner, though not necessarily a faster one. As in the case of older versus younger horses, I tend to go with a ridgling's past performances in deciding whether to bet on him. If those past performances show more than the usual inconsistency, I'll go with a colt or gelding instead.

To geld or not to geld. This is the decision faced by hundreds of trainers and horse-owners annually. It's a tough decision for purely humanitarian reasons. It's becoming tougher as the breeding value of top male horses continues to rise. The owner must decide if his colt's improvement as a racer through gelding will offset the loss of whatever value he might have as a stallion.

The decision on gelding a colt depends on the way he performs in his workouts and races and the way he behaves around the barn. Some colts are bothered by sex more than others. They will sulk, work erratically, leap at female ponies and generally be unmanageable. These "problem" horses that otherwise show some racing potential are the ones selected for gelding. Geldings have been among the great racers. Kelso, the biggest money-winner of all time, was one. The great Exterminator, who raced between 1917 and 1924, was another. Armed, who defeated Assault in the famous 1947 match race at Belmont Park, was a third. Gelding, in itself, has no magical quality, but on the whole geldings run more consistently than colts. The good geldings will certainly race for more years, and the public benefits from this.

Condition of the Horse

Most of the observation that comes into play in betting takes place in the fifteen minutes or so in which the horses are on display before the start of each race. Before a race is run the horses will be paraded briefly in the paddock. Then they will be led out onto the track and be walked back and forth once in front of the grandstand. Finally, they will work out on the track for a few minutes before going to the post.

There are several things to look for while the horses parade. Quickly check the condition of their coats. A sleek, glossy coat is a sign of good health. If the coat is dull and lifeless, the horse is in bad shape. You won't find many dull coats on racing horses, but it's something you must watch for.

Then check the areas just in front of the horses' flanks (upper part of the hindlegs) for signs of "gutting." This is a sharp indentation in the body that indicates tiredness and loss of weight.

Gutting can come from one especially hard race or from too many races in a brief period of time. Gutting is a bad sign.

Some skinny horses always tend to look gutted. Here, you must remember how the horse looked the last few times he ran. If he was skinny the last time out and ran well, there isn't much to worry about. Some trainers like their horses lean and train them that way. Max Hirsch is in this category.

More importantly, check for signs of extreme nervousness in the horses. This reveals itself in two ways: skittishness and "washiness." A skittish horse is one who will bolt and halt in the paddock or on parade. He doesn't look as if he is behaving well, and he isn't. Washy horses are a more common sight before races. A washy horse is one that is sweating excessively. This clearly shows nervousness, and it too isn't a good sign. To the novice bettor, many washy horses simply will look shiny and healthy, but a closer look will reveal that this is not the case. Washy sweat tends to form mainly on the neck and around the saddle, while a normal, healthy coat shines evenly. In extreme cases of washiness horses will visibly drip with sweat.

Sometimes washiness in horses merely reflects the heat of the day. This is simple to determine. If ten horses come out for a race on a hot day, and six or seven of them look washy, you can write it off to the weather. But if eight or nine of those ten horses look calm and collected while one or two are covered with sweat, the wet ones are expending nervous energy that can cost them dearly once they start running.

Washiness and skittishness come out especially in young fillies and colts in their first big races. As far as I know, thoroughbreds don't understand a thing about money, but many seem to sense important races from the extra excitement around their barns.

Horses, like people, can react poorly to excitement. In the 1933

Kentucky Derby, the favorite was a filly, Mata Hari. A lot of money was bet on her even though she was a filly running against colts, and her record seemed to justify this support. She apparently reacted badly to the prerace tension, however, because in the paddock she acted extremely skittish and dripped with sweat. In the race she faded in the homestretch after having been in contention early. The nervous energy she expended in the paddock cost her a chance at victory, according to most observers of the race.

Another example of nervousness helping to defeat a top colt occurred in the 1967 Kentucky Derby. Damascus went to pieces in the paddock before that race, and afterward Willie Shoemaker, his jockey, cited that as the main reason for the third-place showing. Shoemaker predicted Damascus would handle the excitement better in the Preakness two weeks later, and he was right—Damascus won. Damascus conquered his nervousness and compiled a record that made him Horse of the Year in 1967.

Once again I'd like to stress the importance of a good memory (or accurate note-taking) in putting your race-track observations to use. Strange as it may seem, some horses are skittish and washy every time they run, and they win just the same. The same goes for horses with soreness or injuries. Some horses, I call them "magnificent cripples," can win with ailments that would take other horses out of the race. Recalling the way a horse looked the last time he ran will prevent you from overlooking some good bets.

Injuries and Ailments

The most obvious manifestation of injuries or ailments in horses, of course, is the appearance of leg bandages. Make no mistake— the vast majority of trainers don't put bandages on their horses for an esthetic effect or to fool people. The bandages are there to protect a horse from injury or to cover an actual ailment.

Bandages on a horse's hindlegs aren't nearly as serious as foreleg bandages. Hindleg bandages are often put on to protect a horse from skinning his ankles on the ground when he runs. If you've ever seen a slow-motion movie of a horse running, you know why this can be necessary. A horse's hindleg ankles give way under the weight of his body and scrape against the dirt. Some horses come in from races or workouts with all the skin scraped off the back of their ankles.

Foreleg bandages most often cover an actual ailment, usually a weakness in a tendon. If a horse appears at the races wearing foreleg bandages, and I know he didn't wear them his last time out, I am extremely cautious about betting on him. I will watch his warm-up very closely. If I detect *any* signs of soreness, I will not bet on him. Given a choice between two otherwise equal horses in a race—one that is running "clean" and another that is running with foreleg bandages—I will lean toward the clean horse.

On muddy days, when I feel courageous enough to stay and bet, I lean toward clean horses over those that are wearing *any* kind of bandage. Mud has a way of sticking to bandages and increasing the weight on a horse's legs. Running in the mud is tough enough for most horses without having to carry it.

Horses can run lame even without bandages. Indeed, with racing being what it is today, most of the horses in the average, cheap claiming race will be suffering from some sort of ailment, and many horses in allowance and even stakes races are sent to the post with soreness. Often the difference between a bettor's winning and losing for a day will depend on his ability to spot the horses that are so sore they can't run properly.

The time to look for soreness in horses is when they warm up prior to a race. First, see if the horse is being warmed up at all. Some horses go to the post in such poor condition that their jockeys are afraid that any running prior to the race might aggravate their ailments. All but a few horses do *some* running on the track before racing. The lack of a warm-up is a very bad sign.

During the warm-up itself, sore horses can be identified by the "choppiness" of their strides. Their forelegs seem to kick out only a short distance instead of reaching out smoothly and comfortably. This choppiness is not hard to spot. If you are unsure what constitutes a choppy stride, ask someone you know to be a keen observer of horses. In a very short time you will be able to identify this yourself.

Some horses are sore when they come out on the track but work their way out of it. Many times you will see jockeys doing an unusual amount of running with their mounts prior to a race. These usually will be sore horses that need the extra work. The important time to look for choppiness is in the last few minutes before the horses enter the starting gate. If the horse you'd planned to bet on still looks sore after his prerace warm-up and you recall that he was not sore his last time out, keep your money in your pocket. If the horse wins despite his ailment, he might well fit into the "magnificent cripple" category. Then you might bet him in his next appearance if his prerace stride doesn't look any worse.

Optional Equipment

Finally, there is the matter of the optional equipment horses wear when they come on to the track to race. The most commonly used piece of such equipment is blinkers. Trainers put blinkers on horses that show they are bothered by challengers when they race. When approached from the side by another horse, such horses veer away sharply or simply stop running. The addition of blinkers is supposed to cure this reaction.

Most of the experimenting with blinkers involves young colts or fillies in their first year or two at the races; by the time an animal is four years old, he should have established whether he runs better with or without blinkers. Occasionally, however, trainers will try blinkers on older animals.

No observation is needed to know when a horse that didn't wear blinkers in his last race is wearing them in his present one, or vice versa. This information is given on a line for changes in equipment at the bottom of each race listing in official track programs. Such information is also available in the *Morning Telegraph* and *Racing Form* past-performance listings. There are various types of blinkers, however, and it isn't noted when a trainer changes the type of blinkers his horse wears. Blinkers can be completely closed, partially open, or closed with a slit that permits some sideways vision. This is a fine point, to be sure, but it can be worth a bettor's time to go down to the paddock before a race and see for himself what sort of blinkers a horse is wearing. If it's a different type of blinkers than he wore the last time out, it could affect his performance. The next time this horse runs, go down and look at his blinkers again. A horse might lose with one kind of blinkers and come back the next time to win with a different type.

One type of equipment that isn't listed in track programs or past-performance charts is the tongue strap. A few horses have a tendency to swallow their tongues while they are running. When this happens, they choke up and stop because they have trouble breathing. A tongue strap is a piece of gauze tied around a horse's tongue and jaw to keep him from swallowing his tongue. A tongue strap can only help a horse. If you see a horse come out on the track wearing one, check his recent past performances. If you see a terrible race among them, one in which he finished far behind the leaders, you can pretty well attribute it to a swallowed tongue. The tongue strap will insure that this won't happen again.

Trainers like to play around with other types of optional equipment. Some favor the "shadow roll," a strip of thick, woolly material that is put across a horse's nose under his eyes to keep it from seeing the ground. It's used on horses that have shown a tendency to jump at shadows on the track. Shadow rolls won't make a horse run faster, but they do prevent that form of misbehavior.

Some trainers like to experiment with different types of shoes on their animals. There's a lot of debate around race tracks over whether horses run best in the mud wearing "mud calk" shoes, which are supposed to provide a firmer grip on a muddy track. In my experience, the type of shoes horses wear doesn't seem to affect their running very much. Some horses run quite well without any shoes at all. Every track has a "shoe board" in its paddock, where the various types of shoes are posted for viewing. Anyone who is curious can take a look.

Let me give one cautionary note about race-track observation. Don't become a hypochondriac who sees serious ailments in every horse that appears on the track. If you keep your eyes open it won't be long before you'll be able to tell the kinds of apparent ailments horses handle without trouble and those that bother them.

The same approach goes for changes in equipment. Rarely do the addition of blinkers, for instance, turn a plodder into a winner. Be alert to equipment changes, .but let a horse's past performances be your main guide in betting.

Finally, horses have names, and it will serve you well to remember them. All too often, people who go to the track know horses only by their numbers in a particular race. They'll say they are betting on "number 6," and when the race is over they remember nothing about him. The next time the same horse runs he probably won't be number 6 and everything they may have learned about his last performance will be lost. A good way to become a sharp observer is to call the horses by their names. I think it will also increase your enjoyment of the sport.

To summarize:

1. A good pair of binoculars and an unobstructed view of the track are necessary for proper observation of the races.

2. Watch the whole race as it develops—not just your own horse.

3. Color does not affect the way a horse runs.

4. Size differences aren't very important, so don't be awed by big horses. Small horses tend to stay healthy longer.

5. Horses usually reach their racing peak at age five.

6. Male horses almost always beat females.

7. Geldings run more consistently than colts. Ridglings are the least consistent horses.

8. Before a race, check the horses' coats for sheen and their flanks for signs of gutting. Be especially alert for skittishness or washiness.

9. Foreleg bandages usually indicate actual ailments. Hindleg bandages are often for protection.

10. A choppy stride in a prerace warm-up is a sign of soreness.

11. Check for changes in optional equipment.

12. Let your memory or your notebook be your guide in determining how horses handle prerace nervousness or apparent ailments. Some horses run well despite poor prerace performances.

13. Don't be a racetrack hypochondriac.

14. Horses have names: Use and remember them.

7

Men and Boys

Eddie Arcaro, one of the greatest jockeys who ever rode a horse, says that the difference between the best and worst jockeys at a race meeting is never more than 5 lengths. I would never quarrel with Eddie's riding ability—I used him on my own horses many times—but I take strong issue with that statement. I don't think the differences between jockeys can be measured precisely in terms of lengths, but every day at the track I see horses win that should have finished second or third, and horses finish second or third that should have won. In many of those cases, the difference is the man aboard.

The importance of the jockey certainly isn't lost on the betting public. If anything, many bettors seem to go overboard on top jockeys and bet on them more than on the horses themselves. They seem to think this is a short-cut to the cashiers' windows. Nothing could be further from the truth. Even the very best jockeys win on only 20 to 25 percent of their mounts, and because of their ability these top jockeys ride more than their share of favorites. On that basis, one winner in four or five isn't nearly enough to put a bettor ahead of the game.

With this admonition in mind, however, the jockey should definitely figure into your handicapping calculations. As I've emphasized, horses are inconsistent and often unwilling animals that must be urged to do their best. This is the jockey's job. He urges his mounts with his hands, his legs, his whip, the manner in which he "sits" and, most important, with his acumen in judging pace. Make no mistake about it—even the best jockey can't make a poor horse win. But a top jockey rarely loses when he has the best mount.

Because jockeys are so small physically, the average race-goer has trouble picturing them as the athletes they really are. They must keep in top physical condition, and the conscientious jockeys do this by swimming, running and weightlifting. They develop agility by playing ping-pong and handball. Their legs are all-important. It may look as if jockeys sit on their mounts, but they don't; they are crouched on their legs throughout a race. With jockeys, as with other athletes, it's the legs and reflexes that wear out first.

Just about every jockey is sensitive about his small size and a lot of them will go to great lengths to assert their manhood. Many jockeys are clean-livers, of course, but there are always plenty around to uphold the reputation of the profession by having a good time whenever the occasion presents itself.

It was in the late 1940s that R. J. "Bobby" Martin rode for me. Bobby was a tremendous jockey—a fine athlete—but he had a strong playboy streak in him. He was also a heavy and unwise bettor. Eventually he was ruled off the tracks on charges of betting against one of his own mounts, but this was after he left me. I'd always liked Bobby, and in Florida in the winter of 1948 I had a long talk with him. I told him I thought he had a world of ability and that if he'd keep his mind on his rides he'd be a millionaire in no time flat. He agreed to take things seriously, so I took out a "call" on him, which meant Carolyn-K Stable had first option on his services. To make sure he kept out of trouble, I moved him into my house in Miami Springs.

Everything was fine for a couple of months. Bobby rode a lot of winners for Carolyn-K and came straight home from the track. He did his racing homework and kept himself fit. One Friday night, however, this regimen apparently became too much for him. He excused himself after dinner to go out and buy a magazine. By the next morning he still hadn't returned.

Bobby was scheduled to ride three mounts for me that day, but when he wasn't home by 10 A.M. it seemed unlikely he'd be in any shape to ride. I went out to the track fully intending to scatch him and find another rider. I reached the track office just in time to receive a phone call from Bobby. "Don't scratch me, I'm fine," he said. "I'll be at the track in time to ride."

It was pretty late and I didn't really want to go to the trouble of lining up another jockey, so I went along with Bobby. When he finally showed up, about 45 minutes before his first race, I was sure I'd done the wrong thing. He looked terrible. His eyes were baggy and bloodshot, and he couldn't seem to get enough water. I didn't see how he could climb on a horse, much less ride one. But he insisted he could ride, and I shrugged and went up to my box to watch the show.

Bobby won all three of his races that day, astounding me and everyone else who saw him roll in.

Jockeys are employed differently from most other athletes. Except for the few riders who are under contract to large stables, they are hired by the mount—one mount at a time. This means that besides being good riders, jockeys also must be nice to owners and trainers. And being nice usually means telling people what they want to hear.

You can criticize a horse-owner's wife before you can knock his horse. When a race is over and a horse has lost, the owner can't get down fast enough to ask the jockey what went wrong. The horse might be a pure piece of garbage that doesn't belong on a track, but it's not diplomatic for a jockey to say that. Instead, the average jockey will give some excuse such as, "We got bumped off stride at the gate," or "We ran into a lot of interference out there." That makes the owner happy and he'll use the jockey again.

One jockey who never learned diplomacy and suffered for it was Bill Hartack. I was closely associated with Bill during the early part of his career. In my opinion he could have been the best jockey who ever lived. Even with all of Bill's troubles, his record is tremendous. In his fifteen years on the tracks through 1967, he rode 3,745 winners. By comparison, it took the great Eddie Arcaro thirty-one years to ride 4,779 winners, and during much of his career Eddie had his pick of mounts in a way that Bill never did.

In four years—1955, 1956, 1957 and 1960—Hartack rode more winners than any other U.S. jockey. In 1956 and 1957, he was America's top money-winning jockey. He also rode four Kentucky Derby winners. He has earned well over $2,000,000 in his career to date. As long as Bill was winning, he was given more than enough good horses to ride. But when he went into a decline he was pretty much cut off by people he'd hurt when he was on top. Bill's "crime" was his outspoken honesty. A few people have said that he became outspoken and even opinionated because of his association with me, but this isn't so. He had those characteristics from the very first day I met him.

Many jockeys, for instance, put up with being called a "boy" or being given a diminutive nickname, but never Hartack. He always hated the nickname "Willie" that some sportswriters insisted upon. He felt he was a man doing a man's work, which he was. He was Bill.

I first met Hartack in the spring of 1953 when I'd brought my stable from Florida to Bowie. Racing didn't start there until the following Monday, so I took a busman's holiday and went to the races at Charles Town, West Virginia. I've always liked Charles Town because it's a small track where the spectator is close to the horses and riders. You see everything there. I had read in the papers that an apprentice jockey named W. Hartack had been riding an extraordinary number of winners at Charles Town, and that day I saw why. He didn't ride any winners but he looked very good. Every one of his three mounts should have been beaten by a city block, but he got them all into contention. Bill wasn't a "picture" rider by any means. Unlike most top jockeys he rode with his stirrups very long on the horse, and he held the reins loose instead of tight. But I could tell he had a way with horses. I stayed for the Saturday races, and saw him win two of three.

On the opening day at Bowie, the horse Ayem was entered in the first race. I'd planned to use apprentice jockey Bernard Hewitt on her, but the trainer who held Hewitt's contract entered a horse in that race at the last minute, so I was without a rider. At about 7:15 A.M. I was at my barn when a beat-up old car pulled up and a little fellow in dirty blue dungarees hopped out. It was Hartack.

"Mr. Lewin?" he said. "I'm Bill Hartack. I understand you don't have a rider in the first race. I'd like to ride your horse."

Ayem was a bum—a very cheap horse. She ran in $2,500 claiming races and had never been in the money. I told him how bad she was and asked why in the world he wanted to make his major track debut on such a poor horse. He said he'd been following my stable in the newspapers and thought it was a good one. He figured that if he got close with Ayem I might let him ride some of our other horses. That made sense to me. I told him to sign himself on as the horse's rider.

Ayem didn't just get close in that race—she won. I immediately became Bill's No. 1 fan, and I rode him every chance I got. He won with eight of the first ten horses I put him on.

A lot of people have accused Hartack of being "cocky," but he wasn't that way in his first few years. After the 1953 Bowie spring meeting he went to New Jersey, where he rode plenty of winners. But after Jersey I couldn't persuade him to come to Florida for the winter. He said he felt he wasn't ready to compete with the good jockeys down there, and he thought more seasoning at Charles Town would help him. He was right. The next year he was truly ready for the big time. He came back a complete rider.

Bill still lacked confidence in himself for some years thereafter. In 1955, when he was battling Willie Shoemaker for top-rider honors, I got a call from him in Chicago. He said that he felt he was doing things wrong and not winning as he should, and he wanted my advice. All Bill needed, really, was someone to tell him how good he was. I went to Chicago and gave him pep talks every day for a couple of weeks. He went on to beat Shoemaker in Chicago and wound up the year as the top rider.

Hartack threw himself into jockeying more completely than any man I've ever seen. With my help he became a close student of pace and form. He'd study the horses every night in the newspapers, trying to learn how they ran best. When he was in a race, he wanted to know the strong and weak points of all his competitors. He studied the racing papers as if he were in college and they were his textbooks.

Just how smart and alert a rider Hartack was became known in the 1957 Kentucky Derby. Bill was working for Calumet Farm that year, and Calumet's top Derby prospect was the colt General Duke. If Calumet had sent General Duke to the post, Bill would have been on him. A few weeks before the race, however, General Duke sustained a serious injury. Calumet and Bill had to fall back on their second-best three-year-old colt, Iron Liege.

With General Duke scratched, Gallant Man looked like the best horse in the field. Willie Shoemaker was in Gallant Man's saddle, and the combination seemed unbeatable. For the first mile of the 1¼-mile race, it continued to look that way. Gallant Man held a commanding lead going into the stretch.

Hartack knew that Iron Liege was a confirmed rail-runner and he held him in there all the way, saving ground. In the homestretch Gallant Man began to tire and Bill and Iron Liege went right after him. It was then that the controversial part of the race occurred. With Gallant Man tiring only a short distance from the finish, Shoemaker stood up in the saddle as at the end of a race. Bill drove Iron Liege past him and barely beat him to the wire.

After the race it was widely written that Shoemaker blundered by standing up on Gallant Man, but I strongly suspect that this wasn't the case. I think that Shoemaker, knowing he didn't have much horse left under him, stood up in an attempt to decoy Hartack into thinking the race was over and Gallant Man had won. Shoemaker didn't catch Bill asleep and thus lost. I may be wrong in this interpretation, but you can't convince me that Shoemaker, a great rider who had won the Derby two years before on Swaps, didn't know where the finish line was.

Once Hartack had established confidence in himself, his honesty began to come out more freely. It didn't sit well with a lot of people. If he rode a bad horse in a race and his owner asked why he didn't win, he'd tell the owner exactly what he thought of the animal. Bill didn't alibi his losses—he wanted badly to win with every mount and was sore as hell at himself when he lost. But if he believed the horse was to blame, he had no hesitation about saying so.

Bill often fought with the press. If a newspaperman asked a question that Bill thought was stupid, he'd tell him so. A lot of times he was just plain rude about it, and the reporter was justified in getting angry. Still, most members of the press never made an effort to understand Hartack. Bill and the newspapers got off to a bad start over that "Willie" business, and Bill proceeded to take badly any criticism of his rides that he read in the papers. His attitude was that he knew more about racing than the newspapermen so they had no business criticizing him. Sometimes when Bill won a big race he wouldn't even stay around to discuss it with the reporters. He'd satisfied himself, and that was enough. It wasn't enough, of course. When Bill made it tough for the newsmen to do their jobs, they made it tough for him. Nobody wins fighting the press, and Bill was no exception.

Bill, however, had a lot of consideration for the racing public, and he showed it in ways other than the usual waving and smiling at the crowds. When Bill came out on a track with a horse, he thought that horse belonged to the people who had bet on him, and he always tried to give those people a fair shake. Bill was one of the few jockeys who regularly refused to take to the post horses that warmed up lame. In insisting that lame horses be scratched he did a great service to racing, even though his usual lack of diplomacy in doing it made him look like a primadonna.

One Saturday in 1959 at Hialeah Park, Bill was on Greek Circle, the favorite in the feature race. Bill took him out to the track and galloped him around, then galloped him over to the track veterinarian and told him Greek Circle was too sore to race. After a brief argument, the horse was scratched. What an uproar there was! The track was angry at Bill because it had to refund all the money bet on Greek Circle. Believe it or not, some of the people who had bet on Greek Circle were also sore at him. You'd think they would be grateful that he helped save their money, but they weren't. Who can understand bettors?

It wasn't long afterward that Bill did the same thing with another horse. This time the trainer insisted that his horse be run and got another rider to replace Hartack. The horse started that race, but he didn't finish it. From that day on, trainers didn't argue with Bill on scratching horses Bill thought were lame, but they didn't love him for it. No one likes to be made to look like a chump in public, and some of those trainers paid him back later.

Bill certainly was no saint. He didn't seem to realize how much some of his outbursts hurt people, even though they were based on facts. Yet, with people he knew well he was kind and generous. When he'd established himself as a top rider, he sold his contract and gave all the money—I think it was about $30,000—to Junie Corbin, the West Virginia trainer who gave him his start in racing. He built a fine house for his father with his first important earnings. He put his sister through college. Those were the kinds of things he didn't talk about publicly. Bill was a fine athlete. If he had learned to keep his mouth shut at the right time, there's no telling how far he would have gone.

What made Hartack such a fine rider? For one thing, his brain. He did his homework and was a fine judge of pace. If a horse had to have a 5-length lead at the first quarter-mile to win, Bill would get him that or better. If his horse had to have the rail like Iron Liege did, he'd get him that. He had a clock in his head; he knew where he was and how fast he was going at every stage of a race.

Bill was a fine post rider. He would sit very still on his mount in the gate, giving him no cause for anxiety. Some jockeys try to anticipate the opening of the gate, guess wrong, and put their horses off stride. Bill would break even late-running horses quickly so that they wouldn't have the added disadvantage of a slow start. He had no fear. If he saw an opening, no matter how small, he'd get his horse through it. He anticipated trouble and interference during a race, and he avoided it. Bill was a jockey for all horses. Speed horses, late-runners—on fast or muddy tracks —it didn't matter to him. Your money was safe with Bill Hartack.

Everything I've said about Hartack's qualities as a rider apply even more to Willie Shoemaker. In sheer riding ability he and Hartack were about equal, but Shoemaker had the advantage of an easier-going temperament. Hartack ate his heart out when he lost, and he was subject to losing streaks because of this. Shoemaker has always been able to forget his losses and go out and do better the next time.

If I were a sculptor and was asked to make a statue of a jockey, Shoemaker would be my model. He's a naturally little fellow with tiny hands, but he can do great things with those hands. Weight has never been the problem with him that it is with many older jockeys. Thus he can still ride horses assigned to carry low weights. When he rides, he sits so still it's as though he were painted on the horse. He never gets in a horse's way. Early in his career, many people thought Shoemaker was too small to handle big, strong horses, but he quickly proved otherwise. He was the regular rider of Candy Spots, a giant of a horse, and he rode the huge Swaps to many stakes victories. Shoemaker is a good turf rider, a good handler of two-year-olds and a fine judge of pace. Like Hartack, he has no weaknesses. In ten of the years between 1951 and 1964 he was the nation's leading money-winning rider, and in five of those years he rode the most winners. All in all, he's the best jockey I've ever seen. Shoemaker has been bothered by injuries during the last few years, and his age is getting to be a problem. Although it varies, most jockeys are at their peak between the ages of twenty-five and thirty-two and Willie is several years older.

Today there is a young group that doesn't give away much to Shoemaker and Hartack when it comes to ability. Most of them are Latin Americans, and they've been dominating the winners' circles since 1963. The best among them is Braulio Baeza, a Panamanian. In 1965, 1966 and 1967, his mounts won more money than those of any other rider. Baeza is very much of a thinking, sit-still rider. He rides all sorts of horses well, but especially those that like to come from off the pace. He's the best rider of come-from-behind horses on the tracks today.

Baeza also is the best mud rider. When he warms up a mount for a race in the mud, he is constantly probing for the firmest portion of the track. He'll put his horse on solid footing immediately and keep him there all the way. This sounds a lot easier than it is, and it takes a jockey of Baeza's talent to do it. He excels on the turf. Many turf courses don't have inner railings, as do all main dirt courses, and this enables an alert rider to save a lot of ground by keeping his mount closer to the inside. The inner part of a turf course usually is firmer than the rest, which increases the advantage of hugging the inside. When Baeza is in a race over the turf, his horse usually runs the stated distance with very few wasted strides.

Baeza was only twenty-eight years old in 1968, but he's already getting a lot of competition for top-jockey honors from two Latins who are even younger—Jorge Velasquez, twenty-one, and Eddie Belmonte, twenty-five. Velasquez and Belmonte are very similar in style. Each is a tremendous rider of front-running horses. The average racing fan might think that it's easy to ride a horse that takes the lead and holds it all the way, but it isn't. It often makes a big difference whether a speed horse is 2 lengths in front or 4 lengths in front at the half-mile mark. Some front-running horses must be held in check so they'll have enough strength left to finish a race strongly. With those that especially don't like to be challenged in the homestretch, the bigger the early lead the better. Velasquez and Belmonte almost invariably know the preferences of the speed horses they ride and handle them accordingly.

It was Belmonte, for instance, who opened a gigantic early lead on High Hat in the 1½-mile Bowling Green handicap at Belmont in 1968. It's my belief that if High Hat had been 6 lengths instead of 8 lengths in front at the half-mile mark, he would have lost. High Hat needed every inch of that early lead that Belmonte was smart enough to give him.

Velasquez and Belmonte are also similar in their sparing use of the whip on their mounts. Racing fans seem to like riders who go heavy on the whip. Ted Atkinson, one of the top jockeys of the 1940s, got the nickname of "The Slasher" around New York because of the way he'd hit his horses going down the home-stretch. The fans loved it because it looked like Ted was hustling all the way. Actually, that was simply his style of riding. A jockey can try hard on a horse without whipping him a lot. With all due respect to Atkinson, I believe that except for the relatively few horses that run well only when whipped, the whip should be used primarily as a coaxer to keep a horse's mind on the race. I don't think many horses can be whipped into running faster, and some will quit when whipped. Velasquez and Belmonte seem to agree with me on this.

Velasquez and Belmonte are both good riders of two-year-olds —which is unusual for young riders—and they are good over the turf. I think they are currently a bit behind Baeza in their skill with late-running mounts, but they will probably improve with experience.

A notch below Baeza, Belmonte and Velasquez is Manuel Ycaza, another Panamanian. He has great talent and is a fine judge of pace. However, his career has been hampered by numerous suspensions, many of them, in my opinion, unnecessary. In the 1967 Jersey Derby at Garden State Park, for instance, Ycaza was on Dr. Fager, by far the best horse in a four-horse field. Dr. Fager won by 6½ lengths, but he was disqualified and placed fourth because Ycaza crowded the other three horses into the railing very early in the race. Very silly, but it cost Dr. Fager's backers dearly, not to mention Ycaza. More recently Ycaza has shown signs of mending his ways and realizing his vast potential.

An up-and-coming rider whose style is the direct opposite of Baeza's is Angel Cordero, Jr., who won more races than any U.S. jockey in 1968. Cordero has great physical strength and is very active on his horses. He excels on front-running horses, "dynamiting" them onto the pace with his constant urging and prodding. He doesn't allow his mounts to get lazy. Cordero is far from a polished rider, but he'll certainly improve with time.

Bobby Ussery, thirty-three years old in 1968, is another rider with great physical strength. He is especially effective in ⅞-mile races. He realizes that the ⅞ is a long, hard sprint, and he rides his horses appropriately. He's also very good with two-year-olds. Ussery has been having weight problems these past few years, and he hasn't shown himself to be a particularly good turf rider.

Another good veteran rider is Ray Broussard. He also has problems making the weight—something that gets more difficult for jockeys as the years go by. He's a native of Louisiana, who got his early education in ¼-mile races at the New Orleans tracks and is very effective in the short sprints. He's a good handler of two-year-olds and a good turf rider. A careful rider, he keeps his horses out of trouble. It's my opinion that he doesn't get as many good horses as he deserves.

Your money is in good hands when you bet on a horse ridden by Walter Blum, who makes up in hustle what he lacks in talent. Joe Culmone seems to do best with horses starting from the outside post positions. The veteran Paul Kallai, a native of Hungary, does well with horses that run on the pace; his strength (he was a boxer in Europe) will push a lot of horses past the wire first from second or third place. Jerry Lambert, who does a lot of riding in California, is a good all-around rider.

It's not only older riders who have trouble keeping their weight low. In my view, my current regular rider, Howard Grant, has as much or more ability than many better-known jockeys, and other knowledgeable racing people also rank him right up there with the very best. However, the lowest Howard can get on the scales is about 115 pounds, and this keeps him from doing as much riding as he might. Howard, who was twenty-nine years old in 1968, handles speed horses well and is especially good with come-from-behind horses. Horses seem to run well for Howard at any distance over any track surface.

All of the jockeys I've mentioned are riders of proven ability. But what about the inexperienced apprentice riders bettors so often encounter in their handicapping? How are they to be taken into consideration? Until an apprentice rides a specified number of winners, his mounts get weight advantages ranging from three to ten pounds. This is what prompts many trainers to use the young "bug boys," so called because of the asterisks that are attached to their mounts' weights on track programs. In addition, young apprentices don't have the trouble with their own weight that some older jockeys do, so they can qualify to ride more horses.

Every year a few young apprentices show right off that they can handle any sort of horse. Laffit Pincay, Jr., and little Craig Perret, who was just sixteen years old when he started to ride in 1967, are a couple of recent examples of jockeys who were exceptionally good their first year. You can bet on this kind of apprentice with confidence, and you won't have trouble finding him because he'll be up among the top jockeys at the major meetings.

However, the majority of apprentices, as well as young jockeys who have recently lost their "bugs," do best on free-running horses that don't have to be well-rated off the pace. Bringing in come-from-behind horses is something that few young jockeys do well at first; this is a skill that comes from experience. Likewise, be careful about betting on apprentice jockeys riding two-year-olds or riding horses of any age on muddy tracks. These, too, are skills which are developed over the years.

A lot of horseplayers put a great deal of emphasis on a jockey's familiarity with a horse. They seem to think that because a jockey has ridden a horse several times in the past, he knows his ways and will do best with him. This reasoning is fine when the jockey has won consistently on a horse; it isn't so fine when the horse-jockey combination has a long record of losses. It takes a good jockey only one race to become familiar with a mount, and the best jockeys can gain the needed familiarity in the warm-up period preceding the race. A change of jockeys, especially when a good jockey takes over from a mediocre one, usually is a change for the better. This is especially true when a horse that has been running well but not winning with a mediocre jockey, or even a good one, is treated to a ride by a Baeza or a Belmonte. Here you can look for a much-improved effort.

The tendency of many horseplayers, however, is to overestimate how much a top jockey can do for a horse. I repeat: The best jockey in the world can't make an overmatched horse win a race. Some of the best betting bargains you'll see at the track come when the betting public rushes to put its money on a "hot" jockey and overlooks the fact that the jockey's horse isn't the best in the race.

In my style of handicapping, I first compare the horses' past performances, *then* I consider the riders. It's only when two horses appear fairly closely matched that I will base my selection mainly on the skills of the jockeys. A very good rider's presence on a horse will sometimes persuade me to take lower odds than I ordinarily would. For instance, I will take odds of 8–5 or 7–5 on a horse carrying a jockey whose skills I trust completely, but only 2–1 on that same horse if he is carrying an average rider. On the few occasions when I break my rule against betting on a horse that goes off at less than even-money, the horse *must* be carrying the very best rider or one whose riding style seems ideally suited to the way the horse runs.

A final point about jockeys: Don't be too hard on them when they lose. I don't say this out of any special sympathy for jocks. They don't need it. They are among the highest-paid athletes in the world; the best of them earn about $250,000 a year, and even the average jockey takes home between $20,000 and $40,000 annually. I'm simply stating a fact of racing when I say that jockeys are too much maligned. When your horse loses, first blame the horse, then the trainer and finally the jockey. When he loses badly, blame yourself for making a stupid bet.

To summarize:

1. Jockeys should figure in your betting calculations, but not too heavily. Compare the horses first, then look at the jockeys.

2. Don't be overly impressed with jockeys who use their whips heavily. The whip is a coaxer—whipping rarely makes a horse run faster.

3. With few exceptions, apprentice jockeys do best on free-running horses that don't require careful rating off the pace. Apprentice jockeys and other young riders usually don't do well in the mud, with late-running horses or with two-year-olds.

4. Horse-jockey familiarity is only a good thing when the combination has been winning. Otherwise, a change of riders can be good for a horse. A horse that has been running well but not winning with a mediocre jockey can show great improvement when put into the hands of a top-level rider.

5. A top jockey on a good horse can be a factor in accepting lower odds.

6. When your horse loses, don't be too quick to blame the jockey.

8

Sam's List

"Sam's List" was a horse Hirsch Jacobs named for me in 1947. It was Hirsch's way of laughing at a "list" of trainers I was supposed to have whom I considered to be less than competent. Back in those days, there was a joke around the tracks that I used a "throw out the trainer" system in which I narrowed the field in every race by drawing a line through the names of horses saddled by trainers whose abilities I didn't hold in high regard.

Actually, I never had a formal list, and I never really made a system out of betting against certain trainers. But it's a fact that then, as now, I was not awed by professional horse-trainers. As far as I am concerned, the great majority of trainers are as good as their horses and no better. A few are worse than their horses; you can give them a million dollars worth of material and they'll find ways to lose with it. A few—maybe about twenty in all— know how to get something extra from their animals. My admiration for this small group of men is boundless. I'll give you the rest for your birthday.

Trainers are a contrary breed. They are stubborn and love to argue. If you say it's Sunday, they'll tell you it's Monday. Most of them would rather be right than win. Throughout the years, horse-owners have found that it is very unwise to give a trainer a horse he says he doesn't like, because that trainer somehow will prove himself right with it.

For many years my trainer was Sidney Jacobs, Hirsch's brother. Sidney was a good, conscientious trainer, and I had a lot of respect for his ability. Before I'd buy a horse, I'd always bring Sidney in to check him out. Once, however, I broke this rule by buying a little black yearling colt that caught my fancy. The colt was delivered to our barn the next day and Sidney, informed of the purchase, was there to look him over. He gave the colt a thorough examination and then shook his head sadly at me. "If I were you, Sam, I'd try to take this colt back," he said. "He's too straight in front; he looks unsound." Horses whose forelegs are overly straight tend to be injured easily.

I thought the colt looked all right despite his straightness, but I went along with Sidney and returned him to his owner. Sidney was right in a way, because the horse broke down late in his three-year-old year. But I wasn't completely wrong in my thinking about that horse because he did win one important race and did well in some others before he broke down.

Trainers like to argue with horse-owners. The one thing the average trainer seems to hate most is an owner who wants some control over the management of his horse. Most trainers think the ideal owner is the guy who writes him a blank check and then goes off to Asia and is never heard from again.

In my view, the trouble with most trainers is that they are dead-orthodox in their methods. They walk their horses one day, gallop them the next and "breeze" them the third day. A breeze is a harder, faster workout than a gallop. In other words, they train by the "book."

The trainers who have had the most success with their animals are those who let the horses dictate how they should be trained. Since horses can't talk, you might want to know how these trainers recognize their needs. Well, horses *do* seem to talk to a few trainers who understand their language.

The other elements in successful horse-training are hard work and commonsense. Good trainers know every horse in their barns intimately and oversee every phase of their development. Too many trainers leave the daily care of their animals in the hands of their grooms. Grooms are a mixed bag. Ask the average groom how a horse is doing and he'll say fine no matter what the actual state of affairs is.

Commonsense is harder to define. Here I can only point out that looks are often deceiving among trainers. I suppose most racing fans picture top trainers as tall, lanky guys from Kentucky or the West, with cowboy hats on their heads and manure on their boots. The men who in my view are the three best trainers on the tracks today don't come close to fitting that stereotype. They are Hirsch Jacobs and H. Allen Jerkens, both of whom were raised in New York, and Eddie Neloy, a Chicagoan.

Jerkens currently trains for Jack Dreyfus's Hobeau Farm, which in 1967 won more money than any other U.S. racing stable. Allen is a big, husky fellow and an even bigger worrier. He is an eternal pessimist who is constantly surprised at the success of his horses. In recent years he has had many fine horses in his barn at Hobeau Farm, a wealthy organization, but he did wonderful things with horses even before he had such riches at his command.

I first met Allen in 1947 at Laurel Race Course, when he was still in his teens. He was handling a horse named Sam Bernard for a friend of mine, Larry Gottlieb. They had just bought Sam Bernard for about $800 in a private sale. The horse had fair speed but nothing more—he'd never shown any particular ability to win. Mose Shapoff was Gottlieb's regular trainer, and Larry invited Mose and me to take a look at Sam Bernard.

We got to the track at about 6 A.M. and young Allen was there waiting for us. He trotted out Sam Bernard, a good-sized chestnut four-year-old, and told his exercise boy to gallop him around the track for a light 2-mile workout. Allen asked what I thought of the horse, and I told him that I honestly didn't know. I was aware of Sam Bernard's mediocre record, and I hadn't seen anything that morning which made me believe the horse was going to improve sharply.

Allen said he thought the horse looked pretty good, and added that he planned to run him the next day in an allowance race against some fairly expensive animals. This announcement shocked Mose, who didn't believe a horse should be put into a race unless he "broke a watch" (turned in a very fast clocking) in training. Mose told Allen he was wrong in racing Sam Bernard in such good company, but Allen said he didn't see how the race could hurt the horse. As far as preparation was concerned, Allen said he thought Sam Bernard didn't need a lot of heavy work.

Sam Bernard ran and came within a hair of beating Red

Herring, who was a solid $15,000 horse. Sam Bernard had never run that well before. Right then, I knew Jerkens had something on the ball.

After the race, Allen asked me for some advice on where to run Sam Bernard the next time. I suggested a $10,000 claiming race. My reasoning was that the horse should win at $10,000 because he'd shown he could run well against more expensive animals, but he probably wouldn't be claimed because the other owners would look at his previous races and conclude that his good showing against Red Herring was a fluke.

Allen ran Sam Bernard for $10,000, and he won. The horse won two more $10,000 claimers before Allen sold him privately for $12,500. The purses Sam Bernard won, and the money he received from Larry Gottlieb for selling him, helped Allen get off to a good start in racing.

Allen won with Sam Bernard by working him hardly at all, but that's not the way he handled all his horses. In 1963 he had a Hobeau horse, Beau Purple, entered in the Widener Handicap at Hialeah, one of the biggest races of the Florida season. The race was for 1¼ miles, and you don't put a horse in a race that long without preparation.

Allen likes to race his horses into condition, a practice I strongly favor, but that winter he simply couldn't find a race for Beau Purple. He would enter him in a race but the race wouldn't be run for lack of entries, or the track conditions would turn up poor. His bad luck continued right up to the week of the Widener, when rain muddied the Hialeah track and wouldn't permit proper workouts.

So a couple of days before the race, Allen shipped Beau Purple over to Tropical Park, where the track was firm, and worked him 1 mile in almost record time—something he rarely did with a horse before a race. Beau Purple came right back and won the

Widener with ease. This sort of training flexibility has been the key to Allen's success.

Allen also has a canny eye for claiming horses. At Tropical Park in 1955, he claimed a three-year-old named Admiral Vee for $7,500, which was all the horse seemed to be worth to everyone else. Admiral Vee earned $315,000 before he was finished racing, and then he became a successful stallion.

Other trainers and owners have claimed horses from Allen, but almost invariably they have failed to match his success with them. At Hialeah in 1968, for example, he put a horse named Beaupy into a claiming race with a $40,000 price tag on him. Beaupy won the race and was claimed. On his record he seemed to be worth the $40,000, but once out of Allen's hands he became a failure. Very few trainers can match Allen's talents and his knack for understanding horses.

The champion claimer, trainer and breeder, however, is Hirsch Jacobs, the little redhead. If anyone really deserves the title of "genius" in this game, it is Hirsch. Through sheer talent he has mastered every facet of thoroughbred racing. He's had more than his share of detractors, but he has proven every one of them wrong.

In Hirsch's early days, in partnership with Isidor Bieber, he obtained most of his horses through claiming races. Despite the fact that his horses won more races than those of any trainer in America in eleven of the twelve years between 1933 and 1944, people said he only knew how to handle cheap horses—that he wasn't a quality-horse man. So Hirsch turned around and started concentrating on stakes horses. The result, in 1946, 1957, 1960 and 1965, Jacobs-trained horses won more money than anyone else's.

"Ah," people then said, "Jacobs can't breed his own winners." "Okay," said Hirsch. "I'll do that too." In 1964, 1965, 1966 and

1967, horses bred by the Bieber-Jacobs Stable topped the nation's money-winning lists. His Straight Deal was voted the best handicap mare in the nation in 1967. Just wait until she becomes a brood mare!

I was with Hirsch when he pulled off his biggest coup of all—his claim of the great Stymie for a mere $1,500. It was in June of 1943 at Belmont Park. Hirsch and I were standing in the paddock (I was on leave from the Army) when the big chestnut two-year-old came out to run in a maiden race. "Sam," said Hirsch, "I like that horse's looks. He's got good conformation and some breeding in back of him. I think I'll take a chance and buy him."

It sounds simple, doesn't it? Well, that's the way it was with Hirsch. He had a knack for spotting winners in the claiming ranks. It was mostly natural, I guess. Ask a great baseball player like Mickey Mantle how he hits and he'll give you some sort of explanation. He'll say that he puts his feet here and holds his hands like this and strides into the ball so. But really, Mantle just hits. It's natural with him. Hirsch could try to explain why he claimed certain horses by mentioning their appearance, breeding and racing records. In the final analysis, though, I believe it was some instinct that told him the horse was a winner.

The next time Stymie ran, Hirsch claimed him from Max Hirsch, Stymie's trainer at that time. Stymie didn't prove Jacobs right immediately; he ran without success in several claimers soon after Hirsch bought him. In one of those races, though, Stymie showed Hirsch how he should be handled. It was one of those very crowded fields of two-year-old maidens—sixteen or seventeen horses were in it. Stymie got off to a terrible start, but once he saw the field in front of him he started to run like crazy. He charged past every horse but one, finishing a close second. After that, with only a few exceptions, Hirsch told his jockeys to keep Stymie well off the pace until the final ⅜ mile and then let him go. Stymie went on to thrill the New York fans with those great homestretch drives of his. He wound up his career with 31 victories and $918,000 in winnings. He was the all-time leading money-winner until Citation became a millionaire in 1951.

Stymie wasn't Hirsch's only great bargain purchase. In 1955 he bought the three-year-old maiden filly Searching from Ogden Phipps for $15,000. That filly had nothing but second-place finishes on her record when Hirsch bought her. Under his handling, she went on to win 25 races and $327,000 in purses. Later, as a brood mare, she became the foundation of the Bieber-Jacobs breeding operation. Her most famous son was Hail to Reason, a great stakes winner and later a successful stallion.

Other owners and trainers have purchased or claimed horses from Hirsch in the hope of duplicating his success, but horses rarely do as well with their new owners as they did with Hirsch. There was one outstanding exception to this, and guess who it was? H. Allen Jerkens. Allen bought a little filly from Hirsch named Birdie Lulley who had a history of taking the lead in her races but stopping dead after half a mile. With Jerkens she won five or six in a row one winter at Tropical Park.

Like Jerkens, Hirsch Jacobs is very flexible in his handling of horses. He prefers to race his horses into condition instead of working them hard in training, but he'll work a horse hard if he thinks the horse needs it.

Hirsch is a bear for work. He's at his barn every day, getting hay in his suits, supervising every detail of the training of his horses. He's a great trainer of young horses as well as of old. One of his horses, Spanish Way, won races until the age of twelve or thirteen. Spanish Way would come up every spring, win three or four races, and then break down. Hirsch would ship him back to the farm for grass and rest. The next spring he'd come back and repeat the performance.

Pigeon milk? Hirsch Jacobs never needed it.

Other trainers have had success operating with different philosophies. Max Hirsch and Horatio Luro, for example, lean toward training their horses heavily before sending them to the races. Luro says that a horse is like a lemon. You get a lot of juice the first time you squeeze it, but less with each succeeding squeeze. You can bet that when Horatio Luro sends one of his horses into a stakes event after a training period, he'll get a lot of juice out of him that first time out. Luro most recently won the Kentucky Derby with Northern Dancer in 1964. Max Hirsch saddled Assault, the 1946 Triple Crown winner.

About the best education a young trainer can have is racing horses for my friend Julie Fink. Julie is not a trainer, so he doesn't advise his men on the mechanics of getting their animals ready to race, but his long experience around the tracks has made him a master of starting horses in races they can win. Julie is like Fatty Anderson in that respect. In addition, Julie is an excellent student of racing strategy. Trainers who are willing to listen will learn a lot about that from him.

One of the most distinguished graduates of Julie's "school" is Eddie Neloy, currently the trainer of Ogden Phipps' great horses at the Wheatley Stable. In 1966 and 1967, horses trained by Neloy won more money than those of any other trainer. In 1967 Eddie saddled Buckpasser, the great stakes winner Vitriolic, who was the best two-year-old colt, and Queen of the Stage, the best two-year-old filly. Altogether, an amazing performance.

Eddie Neloy has the perfect temperament for a trainer. He is able to take his losses in stride, even when they involve his "big" horses. He's rarely upset or angry with his horses or riders, and he isn't an alibier. Neloy is an expert in instructing jockeys how to ride his horses, something I'm sure he learned from Julie Fink. He has a theory about speed outrunning speed, which he has put to good use. When a Neloy speed horse is in a race with several other horses of equal speed, Eddie will tell his jockey to do everything possible to get the horse as far out in front as possible at the start. That sounds suicidal, but a lot of times it works. Those other speed horses aren't used to being passed early in a race, and often they'll simply quit and allow Eddie's horse to win.

Training for Phipps, Neloy concentrates solely on developing horses with strong stakes potential. No owner, no matter how wealthy or knowledgeable, buys and breeds only stakes horses, so Eddie must separate the promising animals from those that aren't so promising. The earlier this weeding-out process takes place, the better it is for a stable; young horses bring top-dollar in sales, and Eddie doesn't have to waste a lot of time training horses he feels won't be real winners. It's to Eddie's credit that very few of the young horses he's sold have come back later to win big races for someone else.

Another distinguished graduate of "Fink U." is W. C. "Woody" Stephens, who has shown himself to be very adept at getting a lot of speed out of young horses. Training young horses for the races has come to be a fairly standardized procedure. First, a horse is taught that his rider is the boss. Then he's taught to come out of the gate straight and to run straight once out on the track. But it takes considerable judgment on the part of a trainer to determine how a young horse runs best—whether he should be taken into the lead or held back off the pace. Woody Stephens seems to have a talent for seeing this in his horses from the way they train. He's also adept at winning with older horses in their first pop out of the box for a new season.

Randy Sechrest is still another trainer who has gone on to become successful after an association with Julie Fink. Julie's present trainer is Al Scotti, a young New Yorker who promises to be as good as anyone Julie has tutored. Al is fairly new to the game, so he has yet to get his full share of good horses to handle. But in 1967, his horses won 53 races in 234 starts for an excellent 23 percent winning average. That compared favorably with other top-level trainers, some of whom had better horses than Al. I look for Scotti to be right up at the top of the lists within the next few years.

The kind of trainers I tend to judge most harshly are the ones with the big public stables who may have forty or fifty horses racing at any one time. These trainers receive fees for the horses they keep, plus 10 percent of the purses the horses win. A lot of these fellows will have horses in anywhere from 500 to 700 races a year. They keep throwing them in, hoping they'll win. They just run and pray, run and pray.

I think it's almost impossible for a trainer to keep proper tabs on forty or fifty horses. Running a stable of that size is a considerable business undertaking, and a trainer with that sort of operation must necessarily spend as much time with his account books as he does around his barn. Thus, a lot of the actual training is necessarily put into the hands of assistant trainers or grooms, who may or may not be as competent as the head trainer. Operators of public stables usually wind up personally training only horses with stakes potential and giving the rest to their assistants.

Arnold Winnick, a man with a world of energy, is in my opinion one of the best of the public-stable trainers. He keeps plenty of horses, but he manages to juggle them well. I think Arnold trains owners as well as he trains horses. He can make his owners feel happy even when they aren't winning. *That's* a real accomplishment.

Arnold can sell horses he owns as well as any man. He'll show me a horse and ask me how much I think it's worth. I'll kid him and say $5,000. He'll say, "You're crazy. This horse is worth $25,000." The funny thing is that he'll proceed to go out and sell that horse for $25,000. He absolutely believes in what he sells. That's what makes him such a great salesman.

Arnold has had his share of stakes winners. Recently he's obtained some good Latin-American stallions and gone into the breeding business. His stallions' blood lines are good; I have bred some of my Carolyn-K mares to them. I have no doubt that Arnold will make a million dollars in the racing game if he can stand the pace he sets for himself.

M. E. "Buster" Millerick, who makes his headquarters on the West Coast, is a good trainer; he saddles close to 25 percent winners almost every year. Max Hirsch's son Buddy (William J.) also has done well training in the West.

The racing fan usually can assume that a recent change of trainers will neither help nor hurt the chances of a horse he wants to bet on. However, if a horse has just come into the hands of a Jerkens, Neloy, Jacobs or other top men, you can look for an improved effort from him. Beware of horses that top trainers sell to others, because they rarely get better and often get worse. One good test of a trainer is his success, or lack of it, with horses he owns. I think it's always a good sign when a trainer wins with his own animals, whether it be at Aqueduct or some little half-mile track in the Midwest.

As said earlier, the bettor can pretty well disregard the horse-owner's name. Horses from the big blue-blood-owned stables often attract more attention than they deserve. Those stables have good and bad years like everyone else in racing. Indeed, the expenses of raising and training horses being what they are, very few stables or individual owners show a profit at the end of a year. The big stables have more good horses than the others because their owners are willing to spend a lot of money on horses that never race. You'll be able to recognize their good ones easily enough.

One owner for whom the bettors should be alert is Marion H.

Van Berg, who has fielded more winners than anyone else in each year from 1960 through 1967. Most of Van Berg's horses are trained by his son Jack. Marion Van Berg doesn't run a lot of stakes winners; he sticks pretty close to the "leaky roof" circuit of small tracks around the country. Yet his record shows him to be a good judge of the value of his horses. If Marion H. Van Berg is at a track, you'll know it pretty quickly, because he'll have horses entered in just about every race. And he will win more than his share.

To summarize:

1. As a general rule, trainers shouldn't figure importantly in your betting calculations.

2. A very few trainers—those whom I've mentioned in this chapter or others you may spot yourself—stand head and shoulders above their field. Their horses should receive special consideration.

3. Ordinarily, a change of trainers shouldn't affect a horse's performance. When a horse is put into the hands of a top trainer, however, you can look for an improved performance. Horses that are given up by these top trainers rarely improve with new management.

4. It's an especially good sign when a trainer does well with horses he owns.

5. The bettor can pretty well disregard the name of a horse's owner.

9

Horses for Courses

To the novice racing fan, all race tracks look pretty much alike, but the expert bettor knows they are not. Racing surfaces vary widely from track to track, and this affects the performances of the animals that run on them. Some tracks are wide and some are narrow. Some have gradual turns and others have sharp turns. The length of the homestretch is different on just about every track. All this must be taken into consideration by the bettor. The need for close observation of horses and weather conditions that I spoke about earlier must be extended to the race tracks themselves. A thorough knowledge of the track you attend can pay off nearly as handsomely as your knowledge of the horses.

In some ways, changes in racing over the past twenty years have made things easier for the handicapper. Racing seasons at individual tracks are getting longer, and this means that bettors have the advantage of seeing the same horses run again and again over the same racing surface. This has provided a comparability of form which wasn't present in the days when seasons were short and horses moved frequently from track to track.

In some areas of the country—notably Los Angeles and Baltimore-Washington—the opportunity for frequent observation is magnified by what amounts to year-around racing. Around Los Angeles, for instance, the horses race at Santa Anita from late December through early April; at Hollywood Park from April through July; and at Del Mar from late July through October. If present trends continue, New York will have the same sort of year-around racing at Aqueduct and Belmont within the very near future, despite the cold weather. The disadvantage of all this racing, of course, is the physical wear and tear on the horses. I don't think the betting advantage gained by the greater comparability of form makes up for the increasing number of sore horses at the tracks, but I'm afraid the condition is here to stay.

It's well-known in racing that some horses perform better on certain tracks and sections of the country than others. The great Citation, for instance, beat everything in the East in his first two years on the tracks but had a much harder time of it when he campaigned in California in 1950 and 1951, his last two years of racing. In California he won only five races in sixteen starts. Likewise, California horses often run into difficulties when they come East. More generally, when a horse is shipped from one type of climate to another, such as from Florida to New York, it's a good idea to allow him a race or two to become acclimatized before betting seriously on him.

What hasn't been so widely noticed are the wide variations in the style of bettors in various parts of the country. Believe me, this can have a big effect on what to play and even whether to play. Take the New York City tracks, for instance. New Yorkers are the biggest favorite-players in the world. When a horse is listed in the morning line at 8–5 at Aqueduct or Belmont, the New York fans usually aren't satisfied until this horse has been bet down to 4–5, or odds-on. In New York you'll find horses in just about every race going off at less than 2–1. I guess New Yorkers spend their whole lives in crowds, and they aren't happy unless they bet that way too.

On the surface it might seem that this favorite-playing craze in New York might work to the advantage of the intelligent horse-player who can successfully buck the tide, and to a certain extent it does. But I think that on the whole it isn't a good situation. I don't preach betting exclusively on favorites, yet in many races the favorite will figure to win and must be bet when the odds are reasonable. But New York fans won't let me bet on favorites because they push the odds down too low. That's one reason why I don't go there very often anymore, despite the excellent class of horses that races in New York.

The exact opposite of the New York betting pattern is found in California. There you'll find great differences of opinion in just about every race. Every horse in a field gets some play from the California fans, and their generosity is at times amazing. Horses that would go off at even-money in New York go off at 5–2 at Hollywood Park and Santa Anita. Horses that figure to be 8–5 or 2–1 go off at 3–1 or 4–1. As far as I'm concerned, California is a paradise for the intelligent horseplayer. I live in Florida during the winters, but every year it gets more difficult to keep myself from picking up stakes and heading West. I'm going out there to stay one of these days.

The sickness of overbetting favorites seems to follow New Yorkers wherever they go. Betting at the New Jersey tracks—Garden State, Monmouth and Atlantic City—where many New Yorkers spend the summer, isn't quite as bad as it is at Aqueduct and Belmont, but it isn't far off. The same goes for the Florida tracks which so many New Yorkers visit in the winters.

The Chicago tracks—Arlington, Hawthorne and Sportsman's—fall somewhere between New York and California in their betting patterns. Favorites in Chicago go off just about where they should, as a rule. One thing to look for at the Chicago tracks are horses that come from Michigan and get a lot of play from the Michigan people. Very often, these Michigan horses will be overbet and bargains will be available elsewhere.

The smartest bettors in the country? They are without a doubt in Maryland and Kentucky. Going to the races is a way of life in those states. Young children learn how to play the horses from their parents. The odds at the Kentucky and Maryland tracks are the truest in the U.S. You'll find few bargains there, but you'll usually get a square price for your favorites.

Now let's take a closer look at some of the major tracks, state by state.

Florida

Winter racing in the Miami area begins at Tropical Park, where the season runs from mid-November to mid-January. Tropical Park is a 1-mile track. Races at ¾ mile begin from a chute. There is no turf course at Tropical Park; instead, there is a $\frac{9}{10}$-mile synthetic-rubber Tartan track inside the main course. The Tartan surface is very firm and impervious to water. I prefer real turf racing, but form holds up fairly well on Tropical's Tartan track.

Because Tropical Park is the first meeting of the Florida season, horses come in from all over the country during the first two weeks, and the bettor is faced with the almost impossible job of comparing performances from numerous other tracks. I suggest that people bet lightly in the early weeks until some comparable form has been established. The handicapper who makes the morning-line odds at Tropical does as good a job as anyone can do under the circumstances, but until December the odds board at Tropical is more like a ouija board.

Post position is very important at Tropical Park, where the turns are quite sharp. At disances of $\frac{5}{8}$ mile, 1 mile and $1\frac{1}{16}$ miles, where the run into the first turn is short, the sharp turns increase the advantages of the inside post positions 1 through 6. Post position shouldn't come into play too heavily in· normal circumstances at races of $\frac{3}{4}$ mile from a chute, but I've found it does at Tropical. At that distance there, I favor horses starting from the *outside* because the going usually proves to be soft and heavy along the railing.

Of the three major Florida tracks—Tropical, Hialeah and Gulfstream—Tropical is the fastest, with Hialeah and Gulfstream about equal and not too far behind. On top of that, Tropical has the shortest homestretch of the three—it's only 716 feet long, compared with 952 feet at Gulfstream and 1,075 feet at Hialeah. This combination of a fast surface and a short homestretch makes Tropical Park the best of the Florida tracks for speed horses.

After Tropical Park, the Florida season moves to Hialeah from mid-January to early March. The racing purses at Hialeah are the biggest in Florida, the class of horses is the best and the track is the prettiest with its pink flamingos and its green, well-tended infield. It's a little less painful to lose amidst all that beauty.

Hialeah's main course is 1⅛ miles around, and it has a true turf course that measures slightly less than 1 mile. Hialeah runs ⅞-mile main-course races out of a chute, while ¾-mile races begin on the backstretch. Hialeah's gradual turns and very long homestretch make it the best Florida track for late-running horses.

Earlier I said that post position doesn't mean too much in races of 1⅛ miles and over, but Hialeah is an exception. There post positions 1 through 6 seem to have the best of it in 1⅛-mile races. Stick to the inside at that distance and you won't be far wrong. At Tropical the outside post positions have the advantage going ¾ mile, but the opposite is true at Hialeah. Give an edge to the inside at that distance.

In ⅞-mile races, starting from the chute, turn that right around and give an advantage to the outside horses. Outside horses generally have an edge in ⅞-mile chute races, but it's greater than usual at Hialeah. There, it seems as if outside horses in the chute run downhill a little before they hit the main track. It takes a hell of a horse to win from the inside going ⅞ mile at Hialeah.

In the early weeks of the Hialeah season, beware of betting on horses that have won at Tropical Park over horses that skipped the Tropical season in order to rest. The Hialeah condition book is written in such a way that Tropical Park winners go off at higher weights than horses that come to Hialeah from the farms. Many of the better horses are given this early-winter rest, and often these horses go into their first Hialeah tests with both rest and weight in their favor over Tropical winners.

Gulfstream Park, where the season runs from early March through April, closes the Florida season. Gulfstream has a 1-mile main track with a turf course inside of it. Races run at ⅞ mile on the main track start from a chute; ¾-mile turf races start from a parallel chute.

At Tropical Park, bettors encounter early-season problems caused by the influx of horses from other tracks. The problem at Gulfstream is just the opposite. Many horses leave Gulfstream to head North before the Florida season ends and are replaced by horses coming to Gulfstream from Florida Downs in Tampa, where a cheaper lot of horses race. The Florida Downs horses have no right to beat the Gulfstream horses but they sometimes do because the Gulfstream horses at the tag-end of the season are worn out from a long winter of racing. Form goes out the window in the final weeks at Gulfstream, so the bettor must take more than the usual risks.

At all distances, the inside post positions seem to win more than their share of races at Gulfstream Park. My general rule about outside horses winning at ⅞ mile held up well at Gulfstream until the 1968 season, when it was destroyed. Future seasons will tell if the outside can make a comeback at the ⅞ mile. Until it does I'll bet inside horses at that distance at that track. That's what I meant about the need to be flexible in handicapping.

Maryland

The horses run at Bowie Race Course from early January to early March in some of the worst weather imaginable. To accommodate winter racing, Bowie's owners in recent years have radically changed the track surface, which has greatly altered the character of racing at this track.

Through most of its history, Bowie had a unique red soil track. When it rained, as it often did, the going became extremely heavy

and horses came along that could win in the Bowie mud and nowhere else. The mud races at Bowie produced many repeat winners. Handicappers love repeat winners. Lately, however, all
this has changed. To forestall winter freezing, Bowie put in a
hard, sandy racing surface, liberally mixed with rock salt. As a
result, Bowie today is one of the fastest tracks in the country, a
condition that definitely favors speed horses. Bowie has gone
from the slowest to the fastest of the three major Maryland tracks.

A bettor should take care to watch the horses work out before
they race at Bowie. The hard track surface there is murder on
many kinds of leg ailments and horses can become sore very
quickly. As mentioned earlier, watch for horses that work out with
a choppy stride, the sign of soreness.

Bowie is a 1-mile track and doesn't have a turf course. Post
position recently hasn't seemed to be much of a factor at Bowie,
except when it rains or snows. Then give the edge to inside horses,
because the track's drainage system seems to steer the water to
the outside of the track. A bettor shouldn't be afraid to put his
money on horses coming in from the numerous $5/8$-mile tracks
in the Baltimore-Washington area. The best horses are usually in
Florida when Bowie meets, so the class of competition isn't a great
deal better than it is on the smaller tracks in the vicinity.

Racing starts at Pimlico in early March and runs into late May.
The track has a 1-mile main oval with a $7/8$-mile grass course inside it. Races of $3/4$ mile begin from a chute. Unlike Bowie's, the
Pimlico track surface is fairly deep and soft throughout most of
its meeting. This favors come-from-behind horses over speed
horses. In the later days of the meeting, before the Preakness, the
track is skimmed and made harder in order to establish a fast
time for the track's top stakes event.

Some years ago the gate in the chute from which $3/4$-mile races were started at Pimlico was situated in a way that gave a decided advantage to horses starting from post positions 1 through 3, but this is no longer the case. In races of $1\frac{1}{16}$ miles and $1\frac{1}{8}$ miles, however, an advantage still remains with inside horses. Pimlico's homestretch is a long one—1,152 feet—and this underlines the general advantage to late-running horses that is provided by the track's soft surface. Lastly, Pimlico's clubhouse food is very good. I recommend the Preakness salad, a chicken-and-cheese affair.

From late October through December, Maryland racing shifts to Laurel Race Course. This track has improved tremendously since John D. Shapiro became its president. One of his major innovations was the inauguration of the Washington, D.C., International, an invitational turf event over $1\frac{1}{2}$ miles that matches the best stakes horses from all over the world. For my money, this has become the most important race in America, topping even the Kentucky Derby.

The Laurel main track is $1\frac{1}{8}$ miles around and the turf course, a very good one, measures 1 mile. There are chutes off the main course where races of $\frac{7}{8}$ mile, 1 mile and $1\frac{3}{8}$ miles are started. The turns are sweeping, so no special advantages go to any post positions. My general post-position guidelines all hold.

The Laurel track surface is at all times deep and slow—even a little slower than Pimlico's. Mr. Shapiro has said many times that he isn't as interested in speed as much as in the soundness of the horses that run on his track. I endorse this sentiment. The soft track surface gives an edge to come-from-behind horses. However, when it rains or snows at Laurel, as it does fairly often, Laurel almost becomes a throwback to the old Bowie. The mud becomes heavy, and horses quickly show whether they like it or not. There are a lot of repeat winners in the Laurel mud.

There is no major-track summer racing in the vicinity of Baltimore or Washington, but two smaller tracks—Charles Town Race Course and Shenandoah Downs—are in Jefferson County, West Virginia, not far from those cities. Charles Town races in the spring and summer and Shenandoah Downs in the summer and fall, bringing year-around racing to the area.

Charles Town is a ¾-mile track and Shenandoah Downs is ⅝ mile around. Tracks that measure ¾ mile or less favor speed, speed, speed, and give great advantages to horses starting from the inside post positions. If you follow those two guides, you'll never go far wrong on small tracks. Charles Town and Shenandoah are two of the better small tracks in the country. I haven't been at Shenandoah Downs recently, but I remember that its clubhouse food was excellent.

New York

Before the new Belmont Park opened in 1968, New York City racing fans had some definite variety in their horse-playing. Aqueduct was the speed track and Belmont was somewhat slower. Allowances had to be made for differences in contour of the two tracks and the way each was affected by the rain.

Now there is very little difference between the new Belmont and Aqueduct. Everything that the New York horseplayer has learned at Aqueduct can be applied with confidence at Belmont. Much of the variety is gone, but it has been replaced by similarities that can only be an aid to handicappers.

One thing I've always liked about New York tracks is the many types of racing they offer. It is one of the few parts of the country where hurdles and steeplechase racing is still conducted. I don't claim to be an expert in handicapping those kinds of events, but I still enjoy watching them every once in a while. The New York tracks also handle betting very efficiently. Belmont and Aqueduct both have plenty of tellers' windows to take bets, and they don't follow the fairly common practice of laying off a lot of tellers on weekdays, when the play isn't heavy. Fewer people get shut out of the betting in New York than anywhere else, and the tracks still are able to stick closely to their post-time schedules.

Both Aqueduct and the new Belmont are predominantly speed tracks, despite their great size. In theory, the long homestretches at each place ought to give some advantage to late-runners, but in practice they don't. Horses in New York go farther on the lead than at just about any other track. It's my belief that some jockeys in New York, hypnotized by the long homestretches, make the mistake of holding their late-running mounts too far off the pace so that their late drives fall short. Many very long races are "stolen" by speed horses in New York.

At "old" Belmont the turns were slightly banked and this helped nullify inside post position advantages. At the new Belmont, as at Aqueduct, the inside horses have an edge at every distance except the $7/8$-mile and 1-mile chute races. Going $7/8$ and 1 mile from the chutes, outside post positions 7 through 12 have a definite advantage where speed horses are involved. Both Aqueduct and Belmont now have sandy surfaces, which the rain packs down very hard. Both appear to be faster on "sloppy" days than they are in the sunshine.

I haven't been to Saratoga in many years, so I don't have any handicapping advice to offer. It's a beautiful track, however, and a throwback to the days when racing was conducted in a more relaxed atmosphere than it is today. The class of horses at Saratoga is always good because the blue-blood owners enjoy spending August in its pleasant surroundings. I strongly recommend a visit to Saratoga.

New Jersey

Racing in New Jersey starts and ends at Garden State Park, near Philadelphia, which has spring and fall seasons. Unfortunately, the state legislatures that hand out racing dates don't include contracts for good weather with The Man Upstairs, so the weather is usually terrible at Garden State in April, when its first season begins, and in November, when its second season ends. In those periods, the horseplayer is faced with constantly changing track conditions that make picking winners most difficult.

Garden State's racing secretary also has problems during those bad-weather periods. Many of the better horses don't arrive in New Jersey until May, and a lot of them leave for the South before the fall season ends. Thus Garden State must run a lot of cheap races in the early spring and late fall—sometimes as many as four a day. When this happens, I suggest that the bettor confine his serious wagering to the other races on the card. Garden State has a 1-mile main track. It doesn't have a turf course yet. Races of ¾ mile are run out of a chute. It's a fairly wide track and its turns aren't sharp, so only the normal post-position advantages obtain. The track surface isn't slow, but it's slower than at either Monmouth Park or Atlantic City, the other two major Jersey tracks. Jersey tracks generally don't attract the top class of horses that New York does, but some very good animals run at Garden State in the late spring and early fall, when the rich Garden State Stakes is run for two-year-olds.

Monmouth Park, near the seashore, is the prettiest of the three New Jersey tracks, and it usually has the best class of horses in the state. It's a 1-mile main oval with an excellent turf course inside it. A few hurdles races were still run at Monmouth in

1968, but I think this type of racing will be abandoned in favor of more turf racing in the very near future.

Monmouth's main track has annually been changed for the faster, but it's still not what I'd call a speed track. As yet no type of horse has a special advantage over its surface. Races of ¾ mile at Monmouth begin from a chute, and I've found that the inside horses have a particular advantage at the distance. At other distances, my general post-position guidelines should hold true. Longer races over Monmouth's turf course begin from a chute, which begins in the track's infield and bends slightly onto the main turf course. This bend slightly favors inside horses. The horses run at Monmouth in June, July and early August.

Atlantic City, farther to the south and near Philadelphia, is the third of the major Jersey tracks. I'm prejudiced in its favor because in the years 1966, 1967 and 1968 I made the morning-line odds and listed my top-three selections in each race in the official track program there. I handled the odds-making and program selections at Atlantic City in a manner considered highly unorthodox. Many tracks don't offer any bottom-of-the-program selections, and those that do usually just list the three horses that are given the lowest odds in the morning line. I separated my odds-making from my top three selections. When I made up the morning line I tried to set the odds the way I thought the public would determine them through their betting. However, I didn't always list my morning-line favorite as the probable winner in my 1–2–3 picks for the program. I picked horses to win that went off at as high as 10–1, and several times I was right with my long-shots.

In 1966, when I first took on the job as odds-maker at Atlantic City, there was a lot of controversy and some confusion about my methods. People would pick up the program and say, "What's

Lewin up to? He's made one horse a 2–1 choice in the odds, but he's picked an 8–1 shot to win." Now I think the Atlantic City fans have come to understand my methods and approve of them, even if the tip-sheet boys don't. I think that picking a few long-shots to win in a track's official program adds spice to the game. I think that Dr. Leon Levy and his son Bob, who run the Atlantic City track, have come up with a wonderful innovation by giving their odds-maker a free rein in making selections for the track program. I'd like to see other tracks follow their example.

Atlantic City has a 1⅛-mile main track and a 1-mile turf course. Races of ⅞ mile begin from a chute. It's a fast track, but not overly fast. Its turns are slightly banked, which decreases the usual inside post-position advantages.

One criticism I have of all three New Jersey tracks is that they don't provide enough tellers to handle bets. As a result, post-times often are dragged out to enable everyone to put their money down. The long delays between races drive a lot of younger po-tential fans away from the tracks.

Illinois

The three major Chicago race meetings—Balmoral, Arlington and Washington—are held on the Arlington Park track. This gives the Chicago racing fan the big advantage of comparable form over a series of meetings that run for more than 100 days. The Arlington Park track is fast and the class of horses is excellent through-out the Chicago season.

I've always considered Arlington Park's Marjorie Everett to be one of the most enlightened track managers in the country. Like me, she is a strong exponent of turf racing, and Arlington runs three or even four turf races a day throughout much of its season. Marge Everett likes to spice her racing programs with

odd-distance races—such as those over 5½ furlongs or 6½ furlongs—and I think this is all to the good. The restaurant facilities
at Arlington are excellent at all price levels. The last time I was
there it sold draft beer—another big plus for the fans.

One recent innovation at Arlington doesn't meet with my ap-
proval. The turf course there now has a railing around the inside,
probably to protect that part of the course from the wear and
tear that comes with over 100 days of racing. One reason that
turf racing is so formful is that without an inner railing, horses
can stick close to the inside and save ground all the way. With an
inner railing, neither the horses nor jockeys are too crazy about
getting in close. This upsets the way turf races are run.

Arlington Park has a big, wide main track 1⅛ miles around and
a 1-mile turf course. Races of ⅞ and 1 mile are run out of a
chute. Arlington's width and gradual turns cancel out all but the
usual post-position advantages. The long 1,156-foot homestretch
on the main course gives come-from-behind horses more than their
usual chance on a track as fast as Arlington's. In all, races are run
very formfully there.

Fall racing in Chicago takes place at Hawthorne, which has
a 1-mile main oval and a small inner turf course. It's a homey
track, not as fast as Arlington, and I've never noticed that it
favored any type of horse.

Sportsman's Park is Chicago's speed paradise. It's a little ⅝-
mile track (no turf course) with very sharp turns, and speed
horses starting from the inside have a great advantage at any
distance.

Kentucky

Churchill Downs, home of the Kentucky Derby, runs two seasons—one from late April to late May, and the other from early

September to early October. It's a 1-mile track (no turf course)
with a long 1,234-foot homestretch but very sharp turns. In
recent years it has become a very fast racing strip. This, and the
sharp turns, favor speed horses despite the long homestretch. I
lean heavily toward speed horses in the Kentucky Derby, especially
when they start from the inside.

Keeneland is a very sporty track where horses prepare for the
Kentucky Derby. It's $1\frac{1}{16}$ miles around, and it doesn't have a turf
course. As at Churchill Downs, races at Keeneland are run very
formfully. Also, the Kentucky racing fans, through their knowledgeable wagering, make the betting formful.

California

Speed is everything in California. The racing surfaces at the
two biggest tracks in the Los Angeles area—Santa Anita and
Hollywood Park—are among the fastest in the nation. Slow tracks
are few and far between anywhere in California, or anywhere else
in the West, for that matter.

California racing fans have two big advantages in their handicapping: the easy comparability of form which comes when horses
circulate among only a few tracks, and the absence of too much
rain or other bad weather during their major racing seasons.

The class of horses is generally excellent at Santa Anita and
Hollywood Park, and it remains almost as good at Del Mar to
the south and Golden Gate to the north. Racing purses have been
growing in California and this has given Western horse-owners
less reason to bring their horses East to campaign. This is a definite
aid to California horseplayers.

Santa Anita, which races from late December to mid-March,
has a 1-mile main track with chutes for running ⅞-mile races

and the ⅜-mile "baby" races for two-year-olds. It has a fine ⁹⁄₁₀-mile turf course.

Hollywood Park also has a 1-mile main course with a chute for ⅞-mile races, and a ⁹⁄₁₀-mile turf course. Like Monmouth Park in New Jersey, it begins longer turf races from a chute that starts in the infield and bends into the turf course proper. Again, some added advantage should go to inside post positions in longer turf races. Otherwise, only the normal post-position advantages apply at Santa Anita and Hollywood. The turns at each track are gradual enough so that outside horses are not given unusual handicaps. The fast track surfaces work in favor of speed horses over late-runners. Care should be taken to spot sore horses on California's hard racing surfaces.

The betting in California can't be beat, as I've said. You can play favorites and still get some very satisfactory prices.

New England

Racing at the four larger New England tracks—Rockingham Park, Suffolk Downs, Lincoln Downs and Narragansett Park—has been in decline over the past two decades. Tracks in other areas of the country have provided bigger racing purses, so the class of horses hasn't been too good. There are still several good stakes races in the area—the $50,000 Massachusetts Handicap at Suffolk near Boston is one, and the $250,000 New Hampshire Sweepstakes at Rockingham Park is another. The New Hampshire Sweepstakes, for three-year-olds, was started in 1964; it's the race that determines the winner of that state's legal lottery. The sweepstakes is run in the fall, however, and by that time one three-year-old usually has established himself as the overwhelming favorite. Horses from New York and New Jersey are shipped into New

England for the big stakes and then are shipped right out again.

New England tracks tend to be softer and slower than those in other areas of the country, perhaps because the cheaper class of horses that races there needs soft surfaces to forestall further injuries.

Delaware

One other track deserving of mention is Delaware Park, near Wilmington. The Du Ponts race many of their horses there, and so do some of the other wealthy horse-owners. As a result, the track is able to attract a good class of horse even though it is relatively small. Delaware Park stages some good races for two-year-old colts every year, along with the Delaware Handicap for fillies and mares and the Delaware Oaks for three-year-old fillies.

Delaware Park's track isn't especially fast or slow. It's proprietors take a lot of care for the safety of the animals who race there. It's a mile track with a turf course and a steeplechase course. The usual post position guidelines hold.

One final word regarding tracks: I've said that some tracks are especially fast and others are slow. These factors, of course, favor certain types of horses. But I don't intend these factors to detract in any way from the importance of handicapping each race separately with an eye to the probable pace. Speed horses can lose on even the fastest tracks if their speed is properly challenged in the early going. Likewise, speed that goes unchallenged will win over the softest of track surfaces. Pace makes the race in California as much as it does in New England or at a Midwestern county fair.

10

Dollars and Sense

Knowing *what* to bet is only one of the two basic requirements for success at the races; the other is knowing *how* to bet. Strange as it may seem, it's been my observation that the number of race-track regulars who are good handicappers far exceeds that of those who know how to manage their money wisely. Proper money management takes a high degree of mental discipline. The bettor must be in full control of his emotions, taking care not to overreact to either victory or defeat. Money-management skills aren't easy to develop, but their successful pursuit will pay off handsomely.

The average racing fan has only the foggiest notion of how to handle his funds at the track. A few swift losses usually put him in a hole, and he proceeds to dig that hole deeper and deeper by increasing the size of his wagers in futile attempts to make up for his early bad judgment. At best the upshot of this sort of betting is an unhappy and frustrating day at the races. The consequences can be even less pleasant. It's well-known, for example, that people who find they must cut short their winter vacations because of unexpectedly large racing losses are the bane of Miami hotel-keepers.

It's not only the novice race-goer who falls prey to unwise money-management habits. A loose hand with the dollar brought down the only man I ever knew who really had an edge on the game. Al Windemere was a New Yorker who started following the horses seriously at his home-town tracks in the late 1930s and soon graduated into full-time horseplaying. He was a big, husky, curly-haired fellow who was always full of confidence in himself. For many years his keen mind and sharp race-track eye more than made up for his propensity to overbet.

At Belmont Park in those days, two-year-olds raced almost exclusively over the Widener Straight Course, a long, straight stretch of track that ran in front of the grandstand. Races of up to 6½ furlongs were run on that straightaway; without any turns to bother the young colts and fillies, speed was all-important. Given the relatively consistent nature of the two-year-old horse, the straight races at Belmont should have been very formful.

I say "should have been" because every so often surprising things would happen on the Widener Course. A two-year-old would win in excellent time one day, then come back a few days later and lose in much slower time. Al Windemere knew that such inconsistencies were unusual for two-year-olds, so he set about trying to discover what was going on. He "found" the wind.

On days when the wind was blowing down the Widener Course, at the backs of the two-year-olds, unusually fast times would be posted. When the wind was blowing up the course, into the horses' faces, the times would be much slower. Naturally, other people had noticed this, but Al made a thorough study of it. He bought a gadget that measured wind velocity, and for several weeks he charted the wind speeds along with the horses' times in every two-year-old race. After this test period, he began using wind-velocity calculations in his Widener Course handicapping.

Knowing which way the wind had been blowing in past races enabled Al to correctly evaluate the records of two-year-olds on any given day. He'd make his biggest bets when horses with unimpressive times posted in races run against the wind were made longshots against horses that had registered flashy times in races where the wind was at their backs.

Al had this system all to himself for several years. When others caught on to what he was doing, they raised a cry for access to the same information. The tracks complied, and to this day, the official results from the big New York tracks always contain mention of the way the wind was blowing. That's Al's legacy to the racing public.

Al picked enough winners to be extraordinarily successful during the period when he alone was using wind-velocity figures. However, he fell so much in love with his against-the-wind longshots that he never seemed to have enough money to bet on them. Al liked to bet round sums. If he had $98 to put on a horse, he'd try to borrow $2 to make it $100. More often, he'd be out looking for a couple of hundred dollars to round off a bet to the nearest $1,000. He always seemed to want to bet a few hundred dollars more than he had when he came up with a "fuzzy," which is what he called a horse he thought was a sure thing to win. All of Al's "fuzzies" didn't win, of course, and it's said he died broke while still a fairly young man.

When it comes to handicapping—analyzing each race for the probable winner—I don't follow any "system." But I have a definite system that governs how I bet my money at the track. It will take some discipline to follow the rules I am going to set down here, but it will prove worth your while. These rules increase my winnings when my handicapping is good and reduce my losses on days when I'm not picking my share of winners.

My overall money-management maxim, from which my specific rules derive, is this: LIMIT YOUR LOSSES BUT NEVER LIMIT YOUR WINNINGS. We'll break this down into its two parts and discuss the meaning of each.

Limiting Your Losses

The first and most obvious step toward limiting your losses consists of deciding before you leave for the track exactly how much you can afford to lose that day. Once having arrived at a loss figure you can handle *comfortably,* make it your business not to exceed that figure.

I can't stress too much the importance of setting and sticking to a daily loss-limit. This will send you off to the track in the proper frame of mind, secure in the knowledge that you can put your money behind your judgment fearlessly, without having to worry about whether you can afford it. Your loss-limit insures that you can lose every bet and still not be hurt.

Setting a loss-limit and sticking to it will free you from the disease of trying to get even late in the day when you've had some bad early luck. Remember that financial success at the track doesn't require coming out ahead each and every day. Nobody, not even the most skillful professional gambler, can win all the time; don't expect yourself to be the exception. If you are losing on a particular day, strive to keep your bets within the range you decided upon before the races began. Sometimes this will remove your chances of coming out ahead that day, but that's part of the game. If you limit your losses, you'll have funds left to try again another day.

Almost as important as setting a dollar limit on your losses is limiting the number of races you bet in any single day at the track. I've said it before and I'll say it again: BETTING ON EVERY RACE IS FINANCIAL SUICIDE. You might be able to get away with doing this once in a while, but nobody—nobody!—can make a profit in the long run if he goes to the tellers' windows before every race.

Now, I don't expect the average bettor to try to emulate Pittsburgh Phil, the late, legendary professional gambler who could sit in the stands for days on end without making a move until just the right set of racing circumstances arose. I'm not that way myself, and I certainly don't expect someone who goes to the track once a month or so to pass up race after race waiting for some sort of "sure thing" to come along. Still, I think that even a once-a-year race-goer will benefit financially and psychologically through increased mental discipline if he makes up his mind to pass at least one race in his day at the track. Regular race-goers should consider passing more often, depending on how they analyze a day's card.

If you do your handicapping homework, you'll have little

trouble identifying the races that deserve to be passed up. In a typical nine-race card, there will be at least one or two races where your prerace analysis won't reveal any clear-cut pattern of pace from which a winner can emerge. Usually, these will be the "garbage" races for $3,000 to $5,000 claiming horses in which the animals' past performances are so inconsistent that they defy rational analysis. The bettor who feels he must wager on every race will have to force himself to like a horse in races such as these. Thus, my rule on when not to bet can be stated simply: DON'T FORCE YOURSELF TO LIKE A HORSE. If you find a race in which there is no horse you can bet on with confidence, save your money. Remember that the money you save when you pass a race can be bet on horses for which you have some real enthusiasm.

No discussion of "garbage" races would be complete without mentioning Daily Double betting. Typically, race-track managements arrange to make their first two races of each day—the ones on which the Double is based—the worst sort of garbage races. That's because impossible-looking longshots can come along and win these races and make big, splashy Double payoff headlines in the next day's newspapers. That's supposed to draw a lot of people to the races.

Track managements might enjoy seeing tremendous longshots win the Daily Double, but I don't, and neither does any other intelligent bettor. More often than not, I'll either skip the Double completely or simply make an individual bet on one of the first two races. The old saying "There's a winner in every race" is true, of course. But it's hard enough to pick that winner in a single race without trying to pick the consecutive winners the Daily Double requires. For every Daily Double winner at a track, I'll show you two bettors who threw away a winner in the first or second race by joining them with losers in the other.

If you *must* bet the Double (I confess I do, sometimes), look first for a "key" horse in one of the two races. A key horse is one that looks like a fairly "sure" winner. If you can find such a horse, combine him with the horses in the other half that appear to have good chances of winning. Say, for example, that you decide that horse No. 4 in the first race is the key to the Double, and that horses 2, 5 and 6 appear to be the strongest second-race contenders. You would then buy three tickets, on the combinations 4–2, 4–5 and 4–6. If a horse in one half of the Double looks especially strong, you can combine him with four or even five horses in the other and probably still come out on top.

If you can't find a key horse in the Double, I recommend "boxing" the two or three horses that appear to have the best chances in each race. Say you like horses 1, 3 and 5 in the first race and horses 2, 4 and 6 in the second. You would bet the combinations 1–2, 1–4 and 1–6; 3–2, 3–4 and 3–6; and 5–2, 5–4 and 5–6. Those nine tickets will cost you $18 in $2 bets, and the great majority of winning Double combinations pay more than that. In any event, try to keep your wagers as low as possible to leave more money for your more serious betting.

Finally, you must exercise a good deal of caution about betting on short-priced horses. Try to make it a rule not to bet on horses that go off at less than even-money. Try to make certain that horses you bet at odds between even-money and 2–1 emerge from your prerace analysis as very solid choices.

Notice I said "try" to avoid betting at less than even-money and only bet at odds between 1–1 and 2–1 when the horse looks to be a solid choice. No one, myself included, has the willpower to refrain entirely from betting on horses that go off at odds of 4–5 or even 3–5, and I'll occasionally take odds of less than 2–1 on a horse that my analysis indicates will have some stiff competition in his race.

Nevertheless, always keep in mind that your long-run chances for financial success at the track are not good if you make a habit of betting on low-priced favorites. The best handicappers rarely pick more than 33 percent winners. As the betting-percentage table on pages 207–208 shows, in order to *break even* on bets at even-money odds (a 1–1 choice returns $4 to the $2 bettor, two of them his own), you must pick 50 percent winners! I don't know the exact percentage of horses that win at even-money or less, but I'm certain it's nowhere near 50 percent. Not only is the immediate financial return low on even-money choices, but you must pick an astronomically high proportion of winners at that price to show an overall profit.

The situation with 2–1 shots isn't much better. A 2–1 winner returns $6 to the $2 bettor. This means that to *break even* with 2–1 horses, the amateur handicapper must bat a professional .333 in picking winners. And even if he does, breaking even isn't why he's at the track.

To summarize:

1. Before you leave for the track, decide how much money you can comfortably afford to lose that day. Don't stray from that limit.

2. Don't bet on every race. Pass over races in which you have to force yourself to pick a winner.

3. Be wary of Daily Double betting. If you must bet it, look first for a key horse in one race that you can combine with the horses that appear to have a good chance of winning the other race. If no key horse emerges, box your top two or three selections in each race.

4. Realize that your chances of financial success aren't good if you find yourself betting on many horses that go off at odds of 2–1 or less.

Maximizing Your Gains

There is always a certain number of people who go to the races, cash a couple of quick early bets and promptly head for home, feeling smug. That evening they brag to their friends how smart they were to quit while they were ahead.

This type of bettor never seems to understand that by quitting early on a winning day, he forecloses any chance he might have of winning the kind of money that's really worth bragging about. My rule: BET HEAVIEST WHEN YOU ARE WINNING. I say this because I've found that winning at the races runs in streaks. I don't ascribe this purely to luck. A winning bettor is a confident bettor. He makes his selections fully expecting to win. He isn't plagued by nagging doubts that can result in the last-minute changes of mind that are usually disastrous at the track, and by the disease of reducing bets because of uncertainty. Winning gives a gambler the powerful, positive frame of mind that will enable him to pick winners by accident, something I've found that losers are rarely able to do.

Equally important, a winner is betting with his winnings, not with the money he brought with him to the track. Once safely ahead for the day, even the $2 or $5 bettor can do things with his money he couldn't otherwise consider. Always keeping in mind his loss-limit, he can "go for broke" with large win-only bets, or he can execute the various "safety" plays I will explain later that can bring a profit even if his top horse doesn't win. A winning bettor should never stop wagering early if his calculations show that there are good bets in the races ahead.

My second rule in maximizing gains is: NEVER ELIMINATE THE "WIN" FROM YOUR BETS. By this I don't mean that you should always bet win-only. I'll shortly explain when to bet win-only;

when to bet win and place, win and show or across-the-board; and when you can bet on more than one horse in a race. But the hard mathematics of betting rewards "win" bets most of all. In pari-mutuel betting the money that is returned to winning bettors comes from the losers, after the state and track extract their tolls. In the win pool, the backers of the winning horse split the money of *all* the losers. In the place and show pools, the losers' money is split two and three ways, respectively. By eliminating the win bet, you eliminate your chance for the biggest possible payoff on a horse.

Place-only? Never. If a horse is capable of finishing second in a race, he is capable of winning. When a horse figures to be a solid second and the odds look right, take a gambler's chance and put a few dollars on him to win too. If he doesn't figure to be anywhere near the winner, he doesn't deserve even a place bet.

Show-only? Again, forget it if you are serious about winning some real money at the races. Of course, the chances of a horse finishing in one of the top three positions and thus rewarding a show bet are far greater than his chances of winning. But look at the low odds you must take: A horse that goes off at odds of 2–1 to win pays at most about 2–5 to show, or $2.80 on a $2 bet. Look that up in the betting-percentage table and you'll see that about 71 percent of the betting in a pool is represented by a 2–5 shot. That means you must bat .710 in picking horses to show to *break even* betting that way. If you can do that, more power to you. But I don't think you can.

Sometimes the crowd at a track will bet in such a way as to create "freak" mutuels—payoffs that far exceed those which are normal for place and show positions. Occasionally, for instance, you'll see a horse pay more to place than to win. More often, however, a freak mutuel will mean that a horse that goes off at odds to win of 2–1 will pay $4.60 to place instead of the usual $3.60; at that price, place becomes an attractive bet.

The trouble with looking for this sort of situation is that it almost requires full-time board-watching as well as a first-class mathematical mind. I think that the time between races is better spent looking at the horses than looking at the odds-board. I could go into the mathematics of finding place and show bargains, but it's too complex for a book of this sort and is generally unrewarding at the track. Moreover, I don't like place and show bettors. I find most of them to be mean-minded drudges and bores. I don't want to be a party to the creation of more of them.

My final rule in maximizing profits is psychological. You must LEARN TO LIKE LONGSHOTS AS MUCH AS YOU LIKE FAVORITES. By this, I don't mean that you should search wildly for longshots in every race; as I explained earlier, you won't find them easily. What I do mean is that you must have confidence in your handicapping and the courage of your convictions. A longshot, by definition, is a horse the public doesn't think will win. When you pick a longshot, you'll probably have to spend the prerace period in the grandstand listening to people around you tell each other how little they like your selection. Many are the bettors who let such talk discourage them from betting on a horse that could have made their whole season a success.

Don't pick your longshots lightly or quickly, but once you find one you like, stick with him unless there's good reason to change your mind. The only way you will beat the game financially is by uncovering those good 4–1, 6–1, 8–1 and 10–1 shots that will make up for the losses you'll inevitably have.

A final word about betting on longshots. Just because the pay-off on a longshot is big is no reason to skimp on your bet. Bet every bit as much on a 4–1 or 20–1 shot as you would on an 8–5 shot. That's important in maximizing profits. Conversely, the surest way to get in trouble financially at the track is to bet too heavily on short-priced horses. The reasoning that you must put up a lot of money to make a favorite worthwhile is faulty in the extreme. If anything, it supports my rule about exercising extreme caution in betting on favorites. When you put your money on an 8–5 shot, do it with the full understanding that it won't make you rich. A successful $10 bet at 8–5 will win you $16. If that's a big enough return for you, fine. If not, wait until you find something you like at longer odds.

Now let's take a few hypothetical betting situations and see how these money-management rules apply. For the present, we'll concern ourselves with betting to win only, as you'll be forced to do if you bet at the $2- to $5-a-race level. It's only when you win early in the day, or come prepared to bet more heavily, that the various combination bets come into play.

Regulate your bets initially on the number of horses that "dope" (figure to win) in your prerace calculations. For example, if you set your loss-limit at $20 and your analysis indicates five horses worth betting, start off by betting $4 a race and stick to that figure until you win. If there is one horse that you consider your best pick of the day, you might want to allocate $6 to him and lower another bet to $2. Otherwise, stick to the $4 limit. One of the worst frustrations at the track is having a horse marked in your program and being out of money when it comes time to bet on him—then seeing him win.

Now let's take a different situation. Say you arrive at the track prepared to lose $50 and you intend to bet on five races. Naturally, you start out by betting $10 on each race. Say, you lose your first two bets and your bankroll is down to $30. You put $10 on your next choice, and he wins and pays off at odds of

5–1, giving you $60 back for your $10 bet. The $60 you've just received, plus the $20 you haven't bet yet, gives you $80 with two races to go. Now, before reading on, decide on the size of your next bet.

If you said anything less than $30, you haven't been paying attention. Betting the usual $10 a race on the last two races would allow you to wind up the day with a minimum profit of $10, but you wouldn't be maximizing your winnings. Having just won, you should increase your bet substantially. If the worst happens, a loss of $30 or even $40 or $50 on the race (the bigger bets coming if you especially like the horse), would still leave you enough money to finish the day with a profit if you win your fifth and final bet.

Let's say that you put $40 on a 2–1 shot in the fourth race and he wins and pays you $120. That sum, along with the $40 you didn't bet, now gives you $160 to work with going into your final selection. Now what's your bet?

You are right if you said $100. If you lose, you are still a bit ahead for the day, but that's not what's important. If you win a $100 bet at any decent odds, your original $50 will have multiplied many times. That's what gambling on the races is all about.

Let's take another example. Say you start the day ready to bet $30 on six horses, and you begin with a $5 win at odds of 2–1. You now have $40 with five races to go. Do you bet $8 on the next race? No, sir; bet $10 or $12. Start trying to pyramid your money early. If you lose your $10, you'll still have $30 to bet on four races. You then bet $10 again, and even if you lose you'll be able to bet more than your original limit of $5 on the last three races. With one long-priced winner (5–1 or better) or two short-priced winners in your last four races, you'll go home with a profit.

To summarize:

1. Bet heaviest when you are winning.

2. Always include a win bet in your wagers. Place-only or show-only betting rarely turns a final profit. Freak mutuels are rare and hard to spot.

3. Bet on your longshots as confidently as you bet on favorites. Bet every bit as much money on a longshot as you would bet on a favorite.

Weighing the Odds

Up to now we've concentrated solely on betting horses to win. If you are a $2- or $5-a-race bettor, or even one who bets a little more than that, you'll have to stick pretty much to win-only betting because your funds aren't flexible enough to be used more daringly. When you step up into the $10-a-bet class and beyond, however, new opportunities present themselves. In the $100-a-bet class, win-only bets should be in the minority.

Before you start varying your bets, however, you should fix in your mind the prices horses are likely to return for various finishes. In getting away from win-only betting, it's important that you handle your money to get at least an even return for a second- or third-place effort, thus preserving your principal and limiting your losses. These "saves" will enable you to maintain your bets at a high enough level to bring a large return when you win.

Based on my experience around the tracks, the following pay-off schedule should serve as a good general guide for your betting calculations. Make a copy and use it until you commit it to memory.

ODDS TO WIN	PAYOFF AT FINISH (on $2 bet)		
	Win	*Place*	*Show*
1–1	$4.00	$2.80	$2.40
6–5	4.40	3.00	2.60 or less
7–5	4.80	3.20	2.80 or less
8–5	5.20	3.20	2.80
9–5	5.60	3.20	2.80
2–1	6.00	3.40	2.80
5–2	7.60	3.60	3.00
3–1	8.00	4.00	3.00
4–1	10.00	5.20	3.40
5–1	12.00	6.00	4.00
6–1	14.00	7.00	4.40
8–1	18.00	8.00	5.20
10–1	22.00	10.00	6.00
12–1	26.00	12.00	7.00
15–1	32.00	14.00	8.00
20–1	42.00	18.00	10.00
50–1	102.00	40.00	20.00

The place and show payoffs are meant to hold under the usual circumstance of the favorite finishing somewhere in the money. When the favorite runs out of the money, the place and show figures for the top three finishers can rise substantially. A 3–1 shot may pay $5 instead of $4 to place if the favorite finishes out of the money and the money bet on him in the place pool is distributed among backers of the top two finishers. Under the same circumstances, a 5–1 shot's place payoff might rise from $6 to $7.80 and his show price might climb from the usual $4 to $5.40 or so. When your calculations and observations indicate that the favorite will be out of the money, you are eligible to obtain some very high place and show prices.

Win-Only Betting

Two kinds of circumstances lend themselves to win-only betting, no matter how big the planned wager: 1) When the horse in question goes off at less than 2–1 odds, and 2) When the horse's record shows that he either wins or throws in a bad race and finishes out of the money (you bet on him because you have reason to believe he's ready for a good race).

The betting aspect of point No. 2 is self-explanatory. The kind of horse I'm talking about is one that probably will go off at fairly high odds because of his extreme inconsistency. This is a type of horse I usually don't bet on; the only time I do is when my analysis indicates that the pace of the race will be made to order for him. Mostly, this will involve a speed horse that shows a marked tendency to stop but is suddenly thrown into a field that is completely lacking in speed. I'll be betting that a race without early pressure from other horses will enable my fainthearted sprinter to hold his lead all the way. In actual practice, this kind of pace seems to come along about once in every fifty races.

To explain why I bet win-only on horses that go to the post at odds of less than 2–1, I'll have to go into a little philosophy and arithmetic. As far as I'm concerned, the name of the game is *win,* and the main purpose of betting horses to place or show as well as win is to protect your principal for future winning bets. Thus if you bet a horse to win and place or win and show, you must be certain that the worst you can do is break even if the tag-end of your bet—the place or show finish—is realized. If you make a small profit there, that's okay. But don't expect to get rich on your place and show bets.

As a matter of policy, the *least* I'll bet on a horse to win is

40 percent of my total bet. In other words, if I have $100 to bet on a horse, I'll put $40 or more on him to win and the rest to place or show, depending on the odds and my opinion of the horse's chances in the race. That means I'll have to get back at least $100 with my remaining bet to break even for that race.

Now refer again to the table of typical payoffs. At odds of 9–5—the next step down from 2–1—a successful $2 place bet on a horse returns $3.20. If I bet $40 to win and $60 to place on a horse that goes off at 9–5 and he only finishes second, I'll get back just $96 (that's $3.20 multiplied by 30). That's not enough to get me even on that race; I haven't conserved my principal. That's why I have my rule about win-only betting on horses that go off at less than 2–1.

To summarize:

1. Bet win-only when your horse goes off at odds of less than 2–1 or when he's the kind of horse that either wins or turns in a bad race. You won't bet on the latter type of horse very often.

2. I always put at least 40 percent of my total bet on a horse to win.

Win-Place, Win-Show and Across-the-Board Betting

As the foregoing should indicate, I begin betting horses to place as well as win when his odds to win hit 2–1. At that level (a $3.40 place return for $2) a $60 place bet will put $102 in my pocket if my horse finishes second. If he wins I'll get $120 back for my $40 win bet, so my total profit for the race will be $122. That's better than even-money (another of my betting rules), and I will have had the added protection of breaking even with a second-place finish.

I start betting horses to win and show at the 40–60 percent level when their odds to win reach 4–1. The show payoff at those odds usually is $3.40 for a $2 bet—the same as the average place payoff for a $2 bet on a horse that goes off at 2–1 to win. At 4–1 to win a $60 show bet will give me $102 if the horse finishes *second or third;* if he wins at those odds I'll get $200 back for my $40 win bet. That's a total profit of $202, or slightly better than 2–1. Those odds look even better when you remember that I will break even if my selection only manages to finish third.

Whether I bet horses to win and place or win and show, as well as the amount I put on each bet, is determined by my analysis of the race as well as by the final odds. If my selection in a race looks to be so good that no two other horses can beat him, I'll bet him to win and place no matter how much over 2–1 his odds to win go. If no three other horses seem capable of beating my selection, and he goes off at 4–1 or better to win, I'm down for win and show bets.

I firmly believe that win-and-show betting is the way to get the most value out of longshots. A longshot, by definition, is a horse that doesn't figure to win, let alone win by a large margin. If he does win, chances are that it will be by 2 lengths or less. More often than not, good longshots fall slightly short after making some kind of bid. There's no greater frustration for the racing fan than losing a bet on a longshot that just barely misses getting his nose across the wire first.

If you bet longshots to show as well as to win, however, you'll be rewarded by any kind of a good effort from the horse. How big your reward will be depends on how much of a risk you are willing to take in apportioning your money between the win bet and the show bet. Just remember to make certain you'll at least break even for the whole race if the tag-end of your bet comes in.

When it comes to apportioning my own money between win

bets and places or shows, I'll generally try to just break even with my place or show bet when the odds on my selection are 5–1 or less to win. When the odds go over 5–1, I will bet 50 percent to win and 50 percent to place or show in order to make a profit if any part of my bet scores. I realize that this attitude is slightly conservative and I won't blame you if you don't go along with it, but it's my view that being right at 6–1 or better deserves a profit.

Two examples will show how this works. Let's say I select a horse that's 5–1 to win and I don't think that any two horses in the race can beat him. With $100 to bet, I'd put $60 on him to win and $40 on him to place. Look at the payoff chart and you'll see that if he places I'll be $20 ahead (I'd actually break even with a $35 place bet, but I want to continue to use numbers divisible by 10 here so you can easily adapt these examples to different-sized bets). If he wins, he'll return a profit of $380 for my $100, or 3.8–1. That's a good return on a 5–1 bet with a second-place safety feature.

Let's take a horse going off at 10–1. That's twice the risk, so I make it my business to have something to show for that risk even if I'm only partly right. I'll bet the horse to win and to show. A horse that goes off at 10–1 will pay about $22 on $2 to win and $6 on $2 to show. My bet: $50 and $50. If he finishes second or third, I'm $50 ahead, which is not bad. If he wins, I'm $600 ahead. That's very nice indeed for a protected bet. As the odds go higher, so will my safety-bet profits. I'll be making money and at the same time I'll be following my key rule about taking precautions to limit my losses.

The form of "safety" wagering that's most popular among racing fans is betting "across-the-board." The minimum amount of an across-the-board bet is $6, and the payoffs are computed by adding the horse's win, place and show mutuels. A 5–1 horse, for instance, usually pays $12 to win, $6 to place and $4 to show.

For a $6 across-the-board bet he'd pay $22 if he won ($12 plus
$6 plus $4), $10 if he finished second ($6 plus $4) and $4 if
he finished third.

Race tracks make across-the-board bets easy to place by pro-
viding special windows for that type of wager. I think horseplayers use those windows far too often. To be sure, an across-
the-board bet offers a form of protection if a horse comes close
but doesn't win. But by forcing bettors to apportion their money
equally between win, place and show, it removes the type of
flexibility available in win and place or win and show betting.
To break even on the tag-end of an across-the-board bet—a third-
place finish—the horse must go off at odds of about 10–1 to win.
At those odds you ought to *make* money if your horse finishes
anywhere in the money. Finally, across-the-board betting dilutes
a win by forcing the horseplayer to take *two* low-odds bets—
place and show—as part of his package. That goes against my
desire to maximize profits with winning bets.

One illustration should explain my aversion to across-the-board
betting. Take a horse that goes off at odds of 5–1 and wins. The
fellow who bet $60 across-the-board on this horse will show a net
profit of $160 ($120 plus $60 plus $40, minus his $60 bet). The
fellow who bet the same horse $30 to win and $30 to show will
have a profit of $180. Say the horse finishes third. The across-
the-board bettor has a net loss of $20 while the $30-win–$30-show
bettor breaks even.

The $30-win–$30-show bettor also breaks even if the horse
finishes second, while the across-the-board bettor makes a $40
profit, but that's all right with me. By betting $30 to win and
$30 to show I'm right twice out of three possible in-the-money
finishes. That makes excellent gambling sense as far as I'm concerned.

The sole exception I make on betting horses across-the-board is when my calculations indicate that the favorite in a race will run out of the money. Taking that big lump of favorite money out of the three mutuel pools will swell the payoffs appreciably at all levels and make across-the-board betting fairly attractive. The 5–1 horse that pays $12, $6 and $4 when the favorite finishes in the money might pay $12, $7.80 and $5.40 when a strong favorite fails. Under those circumstances, the place-and-show returns might justify trying to exploit them.

To summarize:

1. Start considering win and place betting when the odds to win reach 2–1. Bet win and place no matter how high the odds when your calculations indicate that no two horses can beat your selection.

2. Start considering win and show betting when the odds to win reach 4–1. Win and show betting is the best way to wager on longshots.

3. At odds to win of 5–1 or less, I merely try to break even on the tag-end of my win and place or win and show bet. At odds of 6–1 or better, I bet 50 percent of my wager to win and 50 percent to place or show.

4. Across-the-board betting is overused. Consider it only when your calculations indicate that the favorite in a race will run out of the money.

Betting More Than One Horse to Win

Some racing fans, including a few who profess great knowledge of the game, throw up their hands in horror at the suggestion that they bet on more than one horse to win in the same race. Their argument is that when a gambler bets on more than one horse to win he bets against himself, automatically losing one bet if he's right. That's true, of course. But what does that matter as long as he comes out ahead either way? To me, that's the key calculation.

Betting on more than one horse to win can be handled in the same manner as win-place or win-show betting. For example, take two horses that go off at odds to win of 3–1 and 10–1, respectively. With $100 to bet, you'll win either way by betting as little as $12 on the 10–1 shot (you'll break even with $10) or $40 on the 3–1 shot. When you have a choice like this between a short-priced horse and a longshot, I strongly recommend that you "save" with the short-priced horse and try to win with the longshot. That's another example of what I mean by trying to maximize profits.

"I Should Of"

In 1967 a two-year-old named I Should Of made its racing debut. I can't think of a more appropriate name for a race horse. If there's one cry you hear far more often than any other at the track, it's "I should of."

"I should of bet this, I should of bet that." The minute a race is over, everybody knows what he *should* have done. Everybody is an expert after a race has been run. It's only a short step from being an "I should of" guy to one who goes around after the races are over claiming he picked more winners than he actually did. These guys are known as "red-board" winners. There's no such thing on the tracks as a red board; likewise, there's no such thing as red-board winnings.

Self-delusion and alibis for losses will always be part of the race-track scene, as it is in much of life, but anyone who wants to be a financial success in the game must avoid both of these vices at all costs. It's no disgrace to lose a bet or a whole day of bets as long as you recognize your losses for what they are and learn from them. That's the most important part of the education of a horseplayer.

Appendix

Betting-Percentage Table

ODDS TO WIN	% OF POOL (to nearest 1%)
1–10	91%
1–5	83
3–10	77
2–5	70
1–2	67
3–5	63
4–5	56
1–1	50
6–5	45
7–5	42
8–5	38
9–5	36
2–1	33
5–2	29
3–1	25
7–2	22
4–1	20
5–1	17
6–1	14
8–1	11
10–1	9
12–1	8
15–1	6
20–1	5
25–1	4
30–1	3
40–1	2
50–1	2
100–1	1

Melvin Powers
SELF-IMPROVEMENT
LIBRARY

ASTROLOGY

_____ASTROLOGY: A FASCINATING HISTORY P. Naylor 2.00
_____ASTROLOGY: HOW TO CHART YOUR HOROSCOPE Max Heindel 2.00
_____ASTROLOGY: YOUR PERSONAL SUN-SIGN GUIDE Beatrice Ryder 3.00
_____ASTROLOGY FOR EVERYDAY LIVING Janet Harris 2.00
_____ASTROLOGY MADE EASY Astarte 2.00
_____ASTROLOGY MADE PRACTICAL Alexandra Kayhle 2.00
_____ASTROLOGY, ROMANCE, YOU AND THE STARS Anthony Norvell 3.00
_____MY WORLD OF ASTROLOGY Sydney Omarr 4.00
_____THOUGHT DIAL Sydney Omarr 3.00
_____ZODIAC REVEALED Rupert Gleadow 2.00

BRIDGE, POKER & GAMBLING

_____ADVANCED POKER STRATEGY & WINNING PLAY A. D. Livingston 3.00
_____BRIDGE BIDDING MADE EASY Edwin Kantar 5.00
_____BRIDGE CONVENTIONS Edwin Kantar 4.00
_____BRIDGE HUMOR Edwin B. Kantar 3.00
_____COMPETITIVE BIDDING IN MODERN BRIDGE Edgar Kaplan 4.00
_____COMPLETE DEFENSIVE BRIDGE PLAY Edwin B. Kantar 10.00
_____HOW NOT TO LOSE AT POKER Jeffrey Lloyd Castle 3.00
_____HOW TO IMPROVE YOUR BRIDGE Alfred Sheinwold 2.00
_____HOW TO WIN AT DICE GAMES Skip Frey 2.00
_____HOW TO WIN AT POKER Terence Reese & Anthony T. Watkins 2.00
_____INTRODUCTION TO DEFENDER'S PLAY Edwin B. Kantar 3.00
_____SECRETS OF WINNING POKER George S. Coffin 3.00
_____TEST YOUR BRIDGE PLAY Edwin B. Kantar 3.00
_____WINNING AT CRAPS Dr. Lloyd T. Commins 2.00
_____WINNING AT 21 — An Expert's Guide John Archer 3.00
_____WINNING DECLARER PLAY Dorothy Hayden 4.00
_____WINNING POKER SYSTEMS Norman Zadeh 3.00

BUSINESS STUDY & REFERENCE

_____CONVERSATION MADE EASY Elliot Russell 2.00
_____EXAM SECRET Dennis B. Jackson 2.00
_____FIX-IT BOOK Arthur Symons 2.00
_____HOW TO DEVELOP A BETTER SPEAKING VOICE M. Hellier 2.00
_____HOW TO MAKE A FORTUNE IN REAL ESTATE Albert Winnikoff 3.00
_____HOW TO MAKE MONEY IN REAL ESTATE Stanley L. McMichael 2.00
_____INCREASE YOUR LEARNING POWER Geoffrey A. Dudley 2.00
_____MAGIC OF NUMBERS Robert Tocquet 2.00
_____PRACTICAL GUIDE TO BETTER CONCENTRATION Melvin Powers 2.00
_____PRACTICAL GUIDE TO PUBLIC SPEAKING Maurice Forley 2.00
_____7 DAYS TO FASTER READING William S. Schaill 2.00
_____SONGWRITERS RHYMING DICTIONARY Jane Shaw Whitfield 4.00
_____SPELLING MADE EASY Lester D. Basch & Dr. Milton Finkelstein 2.00
_____STUDENT'S GUIDE TO BETTER GRADES J. A. Rickard 2.00
_____TEST YOURSELF — Find Your Hidden Talent Jack Shafer 2.00
_____YOUR WILL & WHAT TO DO ABOUT IT Attorney Samuel G. Kling 3.00

CHESS & CHECKERS

_____BEGINNER'S GUIDE TO WINNING CHESS *Fred Reinfeld* 3.00
_____BETTER CHESS — How to Play *Fred Reinfeld* 2.00
_____CHECKERS MADE EASY *Tom Wiswell* 2.00
_____CHESS IN TEN EASY LESSONS *Larry Evans* 2.00
_____CHESS MADE EASY *Milton L. Hanauer* 2.00
_____CHESS MASTERY — A New Approach *Fred Reinfeld* 2.00
_____CHESS PROBLEMS FOR BEGINNERS *edited by Fred Reinfeld* 2.00
_____CHESS SECRETS REVEALED *Fred Reinfeld* 2.00
_____CHESS STRATEGY — An Expert's Guide *Fred Reinfeld* 2.00
_____CHESS TACTICS FOR BEGINNERS *edited by Fred Reinfeld* 2.00
_____CHESS THEORY & PRACTICE *Morry & Mitchell* 2.00
_____HOW TO WIN AT CHECKERS *Fred Reinfeld* 2.00
_____1001 BRILLIANT WAYS TO CHECKMATE *Fred Reinfeld* 3.00
_____1001 WINNING CHESS SACRIFICES & COMBINATIONS *Fred Reinfeld* 3.00
_____SOVIET CHESS *Edited by R. G. Wade* 3.00

COOKERY & HERBS

_____CULPEPER'S HERBAL REMEDIES *Dr. Nicholas Culpeper* 2.00
_____FAST GOURMET COOKBOOK *Poppy Cannon* 2.50
_____HEALING POWER OF HERBS *May Bethel* 3.00
_____HERB HANDBOOK *Dawn MacLeod* 2.00
_____HERBS FOR COOKING AND HEALING *Dr. Donald Law* 2.00
_____HERBS FOR HEALTH How to Grow & Use Them *Louise Evans Doole* 2.00
_____HOME GARDEN COOKBOOK Delicious Natural Food Recipes *Ken Kraft* 3.00
_____MEDICAL HERBALIST *edited by Dr. J. R. Yemm* 3.00
_____NATURAL FOOD COOKBOOK *Dr. Harry C. Bond* 3.00
_____NATURE'S MEDICINES *Richard Lucas* 3.00
_____VEGETABLE GARDENING FOR BEGINNERS *Hugh Wiberg* 2.00
_____VEGETABLES FOR TODAY'S GARDENS *R. Milton Carleton* 2.00
_____VEGETARIAN COOKERY *Janet Walker* 3.00
_____VEGETARIAN COOKING MADE EASY & DELECTABLE *Veronica Vezza* 2.00
_____VEGETARIAN DELIGHTS — A Happy Cookbook for Health *K. R. Mehta* 2.00
_____VEGETARIAN GOURMET COOKBOOK *Joyce McKinnel* 2.00

HEALTH

_____DR. LINDNER'S SPECIAL WEIGHT CONTROL METHOD 1.50
_____HELP YOURSELF TO BETTER SIGHT *Margaret Darst Corbett* 3.00
_____HOW TO IMPROVE YOUR VISION *Dr. Robert A. Kraskin* 2.00
_____HOW YOU CAN STOP SMOKING PERMANENTLY *Ernest Caldwell* 2.00
_____LSD — THE AGE OF MIND *Bernard Roseman* 2.00
_____MIND OVER PLATTER *Peter G. Lindner, M.D.* 2.00
_____NATURE'S WAY TO NUTRITION & VIBRANT HEALTH *Robert Scrutton* 3.00
_____NEW CARBOHYDRATE DIET COUNTER *Patti Lopez-Pereira* 1.00
_____PSYCHEDELIC ECSTASY *William Marshall & Gilbert W. Taylor* 2.00
_____YOU CAN LEARN TO RELAX *Dr. Samuel Gutwirth* 2.00
_____YOUR ALLERGY—What To Do About It *Allan Knight, M.D.* 2.00

HOBBIES

_____BATON TWIRLING — A Complete Illustrated Guide *Doris Wheelus* 4.00
_____BEACHCOMBING FOR BEGINNERS *Norman Hickin* 2.00
_____BLACKSTONE'S MODERN CARD TRICKS *Harry Blackstone* 2.00
_____BLACKSTONE'S SECRETS OF MAGIC *Harry Blackstone* 2.00
_____COIN COLLECTING FOR BEGINNERS *Burton Hobson & Fred Reinfeld* 2.00
_____ENTERTAINING WITH ESP *Tony 'Doc' Shiels* 2.00
_____400 FASCINATING MAGIC TRICKS YOU CAN DO *Howard Thurston* 3.00
_____GOULD'S GOLD & SILVER GUIDE TO COINS *Maurice Gould* 2.00
_____HOW I TURN JUNK INTO FUN AND PROFIT *Sari* 3.00
_____HOW TO WRITE A HIT SONG & SELL IT *Tommy Boyce* 7.00
_____JUGGLING MADE EASY *Rudolf Dittrich* 2.00
_____MAGIC MADE EASY *Byron Wels* 2.00
_____SEW SIMPLY, SEW RIGHT *Mini Rhea & F. Leighton* 2.00
_____STAMP COLLECTING FOR BEGINNERS *Burton Hobson* 2.00
_____STAMP COLLECTING FOR FUN & PROFIT *Frank Cetin* 2.00

HORSE PLAYERS' WINNING GUIDES

_____BETTING HORSES TO WIN *Les Conklin* 2.00
_____ELIMINATE THE LOSERS *Bob McKnight* 2.00
_____HOW TO PICK WINNING HORSES *Bob McKnight* 2.00
_____HOW TO WIN AT THE RACES *Sam (The Genius) Lewin* 3.00
_____HOW YOU CAN BEAT THE RACES *Jack Kavanagh* 2.00
_____MAKING MONEY AT THE RACES *David Barr* 2.00
_____PAYDAY AT THE RACES *Les Conklin* 2.00
_____SMART HANDICAPPING MADE EASY *William Bauman* 2.00
_____SUCCESS AT THE HARNESS RACES *Barry Meadow* 2.50
. _____WINNING AT THE HARNESS RACES—An Expert's Guide *Nick Cammarano* 2.50

HUMOR

_____BILL BALLANCE HANDBOOK OF NIFTY MOVES *Bill Ballance* 3.00
_____HOW TO BE A COMEDIAN FOR FUN & PROFIT *King & Laufer* 2.00
_____JOKE TELLER'S HANDBOOK *Bob Orben* 3.00

HYPNOTISM

_____ADVANCED TECHNIQUES OF HYPNOSIS *Melvin Powers* 2.00
_____CHILDBIRTH WITH HYPNOSIS *William S. Kroger, M.D.* 3.00
_____HOW TO SOLVE YOUR SEX PROBLEMS
    WITH SELF-HYPNOSIS *Frank S. Caprio, M.D.* 2.00
_____HOW TO STOP SMOKING THRU SELF-HYPNOSIS *Leslie M. LeCron* 2.00
_____HOW TO USE AUTO-SUGGESTION EFFECTIVELY *John Duckworth* 2.00
_____HOW YOU CAN BOWL BETTER USING SELF-HYPNOSIS *Jack Heise* 2.00
_____HOW YOU CAN PLAY BETTER GOLF USING SELF-HYPNOSIS *Heise* 2.00
_____HYPNOSIS AND SELF-HYPNOSIS *Bernard Hollander, M.D.* 2.00
_____HYPNOTISM *(Originally published in 1893) Carl Sextus* 3.00
_____HYPNOTISM & PSYCHIC PHENOMENA *Simeon Edwards* 3.00
_____HYPNOTISM MADE EASY *Dr. Ralph Winn* 2.00
_____HYPNOTISM MADE PRACTICAL *Louis Orton* 2.00
_____HYPNOTISM REVEALED *Melvin Powers* 2.00
_____HYPNOTISM TODAY *Leslie LeCron & Jean Bordeaux, Ph.D.* 2.00
_____MODERN HYPNOSIS *Lesley Kuhn & Salvatore Russo, Ph.D.* 4.00
_____NEW CONCEPTS OF HYPNOSIS *Bernard C. Gindes, M.D.* 4.00
_____POST-HYPNOTIC INSTRUCTIONS *Arnold Furst* 3.00
    How to give post-hypnotic suggestions for therapeutic purposes.
_____PRACTICAL GUIDE TO SELF-HYPNOSIS *Melvin Powers* 2.00
_____PRACTICAL HYPNOTISM *Philip Magonet, M.D.* 2.00
_____SECRETS OF HYPNOTISM *S. J. Van Pelt, M.D.* 3.00
_____SELF-HYPNOSIS *Paul Adams* 3.00
_____SELF-HYPNOSIS Its Theory, Technique & Application *Melvin Powers* 2.00
_____SELF-HYPNOSIS A Conditioned-Response Technique *Laurance Sparks* 4.00
_____THERAPY THROUGH HYPNOSIS *edited by Raphael H. Rhodes* 3.00

JUDAICA

_____HOW TO LIVE A RICHER & FULLER LIFE *Rabbi Edgar F. Magnin* 2.00
_____MODERN ISRAEL *Lily Edelman* 2.00
_____OUR JEWISH HERITAGE *Rabbi Alfred Wolf & Joseph Gaer* 2.00
_____ROMANCE OF HASSIDISM *Jacob S. Minkin* 2.50
_____SERVICE OF THE HEART *Evelyn Garfield, Ph.D.* 3.00
_____STORY OF ISRAEL IN COINS *Jean & Maurice Gould* 2.00
_____STORY OF ISRAEL IN STAMPS *Maxim & Gabriel Shamir* 1.00
_____TONGUE OF THE PROPHETS *Robert St. John* 3.00
_____TREASURY OF COMFORT *edited by Rabbi Sidney Greenberg* 4.00

JUST FOR WOMEN

_____COSMOPOLITAN'S GUIDE TO MARVELOUS MEN
    Foreword by *Helen Gurley Brown* 3.00
_____COSMOPOLITAN'S NEW ETIQUETTE GUIDE
    Foreword by *Helen Gurley Brown* 4.00
_____COSMOPOLITAN'S HANG-UP HANDBOOK
    Foreword by *Helen Gurley Brown* 4.00
_____JUST FOR WOMEN — A Guide to the Female Body *Richard E. Sand, M.D.* 3.00
_____NEW APPROACHES TO SEX IN MARRIAGE *John E. Eichenlaub, M.D.* 3.00
_____SEXUALLY ADEQUATE FEMALE *Frank S. Caprio, M.D.* 2.00

_____YOUR FIRST YEAR OF MARRIAGE *Dr. Tom McGinnis*   3.00

MARRIAGE, SEX & PARENTHOOD

_____ABILITY TO LOVE *Dr. Allan Fromme*   4.00
_____ENCYCLOPEDIA OF MODERN SEX & LOVE TECHNIQUES *Macandrew*   4.00
_____GUIDE TO SUCCESSFUL MARRIAGE *Drs. Albert Ellis & Robert Harper*   3.00
_____HOW TO RAISE AN EMOTIONALLY HEALTHY, HAPPY CHILD *A. Ellis*   3.00
_____IMPOTENCE & FRIGIDITY *Edwin W. Hirsch, M.D.*   3.00
_____SEX WITHOUT GUILT *Albert Ellis, Ph.D.*   2.00
_____SEXUALLY ADEQUATE MALE *Frank S. Caprio, M.D.*   3.00

METAPHYSICS & OCCULT

_____BOOK OF TALISMANS, AMULETS & ZODIACAL GEMS *William Pavitt*   3.00
_____CONCENTRATION—A Guide to Mental Mastery *Mouni Sadhu*   3.00
_____CRITIQUES OF GOD — The case against belief in God   7.00
_____DREAMS & OMENS REVEALED *Fred Gettings*   2.00
_____EXTRASENSORY PERCEPTION *Simeon Edmunds*   2.00
_____EXTRA-TERRESTRIAL INTELLIGENCE—The First Encounter   6.00
_____FORTUNE TELLING WITH CARDS *P. Foli*   2.00
_____HANDWRITING ANALYSIS MADE EASY *John Marley*   2.00
_____HANDWRITING TELLS *Nadya Olyanova*   3.00
_____HOW TO UNDERSTAND YOUR DREAMS *Geoffrey A. Dudley*   2.00
_____ILLUSTRATED YOGA *William Zorn*   3.00
_____IN DAYS OF GREAT PEACE *Mouni Sadhu*   3.00
_____KING SOLOMON'S TEMPLE IN THE MASONIC TRADITION *Alex Horne*   5.00
_____MAGICIAN — His training and work *W. E. Butler*   2.00
_____MEDITATION *Mouni Sadhu*   3.00
_____MODERN NUMEROLOGY *Morris C. Goodman*   2.00
_____NUMEROLOGY—ITS FACTS AND SECRETS *Ariel Yvon Taylor*   2.00
_____PALMISTRY MADE EASY *Fred Gettings*   2.00
_____PALMISTRY MADE PRACTICAL *Elizabeth Daniels Squire*   3.00
_____PALMISTRY SECRETS REVEALED *Henry Frith*   2.00
_____PRACTICAL YOGA *Ernest Wood*   3.00
_____PROPHECY IN OUR TIME *Martin Ebon*   2.50
_____PSYCHOLOGY OF HANDWRITING *Nadya Olyanova*   3.00
_____SEEING INTO THE FUTURE *Harvey Day*   2.00
_____SUPERSTITION — Are you superstitious? *Eric Maple*   2.00
_____TAROT *Mouni Sadhu*   4.00
_____TAROT OF THE BOHEMIANS *Papus*   3.00
_____TEST YOUR ESP *Martin Ebon*   2.00
_____WAYS TO SELF-REALIZATION *Mouni Sadhu*   3.00
_____WITCHCRAFT, MAGIC & OCCULTISM—A Fascinating History *W. B. Crow*   3.00
_____WITCHCRAFT — THE SIXTH SENSE *Justine Glass*   2.00
_____WORLD OF PSYCHIC RESEARCH *Hereward Carrington*   2.00
_____YOU CAN ANALYZE HANDWRITING *Robert Holder*   2.00

SELF-HELP & INSPIRATIONAL

_____CYBERNETICS WITHIN US *Y. Saparina*   3.00
_____DAILY POWER FOR JOYFUL LIVING *Dr. Donald Curtis*   2.00
_____DOCTOR PSYCHO-CYBERNETICS *Maxwell Maltz, M.D.*   3.00
_____DYNAMIC THINKING *Melvin Powers*   1.00
_____GREATEST POWER IN THE UNIVERSE *U. S. Andersen*   4.00
_____GROW RICH WHILE YOU SLEEP *Ben Sweetland*   3.00
_____GROWTH THROUGH REASON *Albert Ellis, Ph.D.*   3.00
_____GUIDE TO DEVELOPING YOUR POTENTIAL *Herbert A. Otto, Ph.D.*   3.00
_____GUIDE TO LIVING IN BALANCE *Frank S. Caprio, M.D.*   2.00
_____HELPING YOURSELF WITH APPLIED PSYCHOLOGY *R. Henderson*   2.00
_____HELPING YOURSELF WITH PSYCHIATRY *Frank S. Caprio, M.D.*   2.00
_____HOW TO ATTRACT GOOD LUCK *A. H. Z. Carr*   2.00
_____HOW TO CONTROL YOUR DESTINY *Norvell*   3.00
_____HOW TO DEVELOP A WINNING PERSONALITY *Martin Panzer*   3.00
_____HOW TO DEVELOP AN EXCEPTIONAL MEMORY *Young & Gibson*   3.00
_____HOW TO OVERCOME YOUR FEARS *M. P. Leahy, M.D.*   3.00
_____HOW YOU CAN HAVE CONFIDENCE AND POWER *Les Giblin*   3.00
_____HUMAN PROBLEMS & HOW TO SOLVE THEM *Dr. Donald Curtis*   3.00
_____I CAN *Ben Sweetland*   4.00

_____I WILL _Ben Sweetland_		3.00
_____LEFT-HANDED PEOPLE _Michael Barsley_		3.00
_____MAGIC IN YOUR MIND _U. S. Andersen_		3.00
_____MAGIC OF THINKING BIG _Dr. David J. Schwartz_		2.00
_____MAGIC POWER OF YOUR MIND _Walter M. Germain_		4.00
_____MENTAL POWER THRU SLEEP SUGGESTION _Melvin Powers_		1.00
_____NEW GUIDE TO RATIONAL LIVING _Albert Ellis, Ph.D. - R. Harper, Ph.D._		3.00
_____OUR TROUBLED SELVES _Dr. Allan Fromme_		3.00
_____PRACTICAL GUIDE TO SUCCESS & POPULARITY _C. W. Bailey_		2.00
_____PSYCHO-CYBERNETICS _Maxwell Maltz, M.D._		2.00
_____SCIENCE OF MIND IN DAILY LIVING _Dr. Donald Curtis_		2.00
_____SECRET POWER OF THE PYRAMIDS _U. S. Andersen_		4.00
_____SECRET OF SECRETS _U. S. Andersen_		4.00
_____STUTTERING AND WHAT YOU CAN DO ABOUT IT _W. Johnson, Ph.D._		2.00
_____SUCCESS-CYBERNETICS _U. S. Andersen_		4.00
_____10 DAYS TO A GREAT NEW LIFE _William E. Edwards_		3.00
_____THINK AND GROW RICH _Napoleon Hill_		3.00
_____THREE MAGIC WORDS _U. S. Andersen_		3.00
_____TREASURY OF THE ART OF LIVING _Sidney S. Greenberg_		3.00
_____YOU ARE NOT THE TARGET _Laura Huxley_		3.00
_____YOUR SUBCONSCIOUS POWER _Charles M. Simmons_		3.00
_____YOUR THOUGHTS CAN CHANGE YOUR LIFE _Dr. Donald Curtis_		3.00

SPORTS

_____ARCHERY — An Expert's Guide _Don Stamp_		2.00
_____BICYCLING FOR FUN AND GOOD HEALTH _Kenneth E. Luther_		2.00
_____BILLIARDS—Pocket • Carom • Three Cushion _Clive Cottingham, Jr._		2.00
_____CAMPING-OUT 101 Ideas & Activities _Bruno Knobel_		2.00
_____COMPLETE GUIDE TO FISHING _Vlad Evanoff_		2.00
_____HOW TO WIN AT POCKET BILLIARDS _Edward D. Knuchell_		3.00
_____LEARNING & TEACHING SOCCER SKILLS _Eric Worthington_		3.00
_____MOTORCYCLING FOR BEGINNERS _I. G. Edmonds_		2.00
_____PRACTICAL BOATING _W. S. Kals_		3.00
_____SECRET OF BOWLING STRIKES _Dawson Taylor_		2.00
_____SECRET OF PERFECT PUTTING _Horton Smith & Dawson Taylor_		2.00
_____SECRET WHY FISH BITE _James Westman_		2.00
_____SKIER'S POCKET BOOK _Otti Wiedman_ (4¼" x 6")		2.50
_____SOCCER—The game & how to play it _Gary Rosenthal_		2.00
_____TABLE TENNIS MADE EASY _Johnny Leach_		2.00

TENNIS LOVERS' LIBRARY

_____BEGINNER'S GUIDE TO WINNING TENNIS _Helen Hull Jacobs_		2.00
_____HOW TO BEAT BETTER TENNIS PLAYERS _Loring Fiske_		4.00
_____HOW TO IMPROVE YOUR TENNIS—Style, Strategy & Analysis _C. Wilson_		2.00
_____INSIDE TENNIS — Techniques of Winning _Jim Leighton_		3.00
_____PLAY TENNIS WITH ROSEWALL _Ken Rosewall_		2.00
_____PSYCH YOURSELF TO BETTER TENNIS _Dr. Walter A. Luszki_		2.00
_____SUCCESSFUL TENNIS _Neale Fraser_		2.00
_____TENNIS FOR BEGINNERS _Dr. H. A. Murray_		2.00
_____TENNIS MADE EASY _Joel Brecheen_		2.00
_____WEEKEND TENNIS—How to have fun & win at the same time _Bill Talbert_		3.00
_____WINNING WITH PERCENTAGE TENNIS _Jack Lowe_		2.00
An Expert's Guide to Smart Court Strategy & Technique		

WILSHIRE MINIATURE LIBRARY (4¼" x 6" in full color)

_____BUTTERFLIES		2.50
_____LIPIZZANERS & THE SPANISH RIDING SCHOOL		2.50
_____SKIER'S POCKET BOOK		2.50

WILSHIRE PET LIBRARY

_____DOG OBEDIENCE TRAINING _Gust Kessopulos_		3.00
_____DOG TRAINING MADE EASY & FUN _John W. Kellogg_		2.00
_____HOW TO BRING UP YOUR PET DOG _Kurt Unkelbach_		2.00
_____HOW TO RAISE & TRAIN YOUR PUPPY _Jeff Griffen_		2.00
_____PIGEONS: HOW TO RAISE & TRAIN THEM _William H. Allen, Jr._		2.00